THE PRIMARY SUBJECT MANAGER'S HANDBOOK SERIES

Coordinating English at Key Stage 2

D1350271

THE SUBJECT LEADER'S HANDBOOKS

Series Editor: Mike Harrison, Centre for Primary Education, School of Education, The University of Manchester, Oxford Road, Manchester, M13 9DP

Coordinating mathematics across the primary school
Tony Brown

Coordinating English at Key Stage 1
Mick Waters and Tony Martin

Coordinating English at Key Stage 2
Mick Waters and Tony Martin

Coordinating science across the primary school
Lynn D. Newton and Douglas P. Newton

Coordinating information and communications technology across the primary school
Mike Harrison

Coordinating art across the primary school
Robert Clement, Judith Piotrowski and Ivy Roberts

Coordinating design and technology across the primary school
Alan Cross

Coordinating geography across the primary school
John Halocha

Coordinating history across the primary school
Julie Davies and Jason Redmond

Coordinating music across the primary school
Sarah Hennessy

Coordinating religious education across the primary school
Derek Bastide

Coordinating physical education across the primary school
Carole Raymond

Management skills for SEN coordinators
Sylvia Phillips, Jennifer Goodwin and Rosita Heron

Building a whole school assessment policy
Mike Wintle and Mike Harrison

The primary coordinator and OFSTED re-inspection
Phil Gadsby and Mike Harrison

Coordinating the curriculum in the smaller primary school
Mick Waters

Coordinating English at Key Stage 2

Mick Waters and Tony Martin

FALMER PRESS
· Taylor & Francis Group ·

UK	The Falmer Press, 1 Gunpowder Square, London, EC4A 3DE
USA	The Falmer Press, Taylor & Francis Inc., 325 Chestnut Street, 8th Floor, Philadelphia, PA 19106

First published in 1999

A catalogue record for this book is available from the British Library

ISBN 0 7507 0686 4 paper

Library of Congress Cataloging-in-Publication Data are available on request

Jacket design by Carla Turchini

Typeset in 10/14pt Melior and printed by Graphicraft Limited, Hong Kong

Every effort has been made to contact copyright holders for their permission to reprint material in this book. The publishers would be grateful to hear from any copyright holder who is not here acknowledged and will undertake to rectify any errors or omissions in future editions of this book.

Contents

Part one
The role of the coordinator

Part two
What the English coordinator needs to know

Part three
Developing whole school policies and schemes of work

List of figures

Acknowledgments

We should like to thank Madeleine Lindley for compiling the list of books and resources. The service which her organisation provides for teachers is second to none. Nancy Martin's pack 'Introducing Wordsworth: Classic Poems for Literacy Teaching at Key Stage 2' (on pp. 70–2) contains so much fascinating information and so many ideas for teachers. Thanks to the Wordsworth Trust, Grasmere, for permission to print extracts from it.

Ideas for target setting came from Janet Warburton, advisory teacher with Lancashire LEA. Examples of children's work and teachers' planning and practice have been provided by Kendray Primary School (Barnsley), Quarry View Junior School (Sunderland), St. Joseph's Primary School (North Tyneside), Mortimer Road Primary School (South Shields), Lomeshaye Junior School (Lancashire), The British School (Viborg, Denmark) and the Service Children's Education primary schools in Hong Kong. Many thanks to them all.

Series Editor's Preface

This book has been prepared for primary teachers charged with the responsibility of acting as coordinators for English at Key Stage 2. It forms part of a series of new publications that set out to advise such teachers on the complex issues of improving teaching and learning through managing each element of the primary school curriculum.

Why is there a need for such a series? Most authorities recognise, after all, that the quality of primary children's work and learning depends upon the skills of their class teacher, not in the structure of management systems, sagacity of the policy documents or the titles and job descriptions of members of staff. Many today recognise that school improvement equates directly to the improvement of teaching, so surely all tasks, other than imparting subject knowledge, are merely a distraction for the committed primary teacher.

Nothing should take teachers away from their most important role, that is, serving the best interests of the class of children in their care and this book, and the others in the series, does not wish to diminish that mission. However, the increasing complexity of the primary curriculum and society's expanding expectations, make it very difficult for the class teacher to keep up to date with every development. Within traditional subject areas there has been an explosion of knowledge and new fields introduced such as science, technology, design, problem solving and health education, not to mention the uses of computers. These are now considered entitlements for primary children. Furthermore, we now expect all children to succeed at these studies, not just the fortunate few. All this has overwhelmed a class teacher system largely unchanged since the inception of primary schools.

Primary class teachers cannot possibly be expert in every aspect of the curriculum they are required to teach. To whom can they turn for help? It is unrealistic to assume that such support will be available from the headteacher whose responsibilities have grown ever wider since the 1988 Educational Reform Act. Constraints, including additional staff costs, and the loss of benefits from the strength and security of the class teacher system, militate against wholesale adoption of specialist or semi-specialist teaching. Help therefore has to come from exploiting the talents of teachers themselves, in a process of mutual support. Hence, primary schools have chosen many and varied systems of consultancy or subject coordination which best suit the needs of their children and the current expertise of the staff.

In fact, curriculum leadership functions in primary schools have increasingly been shared with class teachers through the policy of curriculum coordination for the past twenty years, especially to improve the consistency of work in language and mathematics. Since then each school has developed their own system and the series recognises that the system each reader is part of will be a compromise between the ideal and the possible. Campbell and Neill (1994) show that by 1991 nearly nine out of every ten primary class teachers had such responsibility and the average number of subjects each was between 1.5 and 2.2 (depending on the size of school).

These are the people for whom this series sets out to help to do this part of their work. The books each deal with specific issues whilst at the same time providing an overview of general themes in the management of the subject curriculum. The term *subject leader* is used in an inclusive sense and combines the two major roles that such teachers play when they have responsibility for subjects and aspects of the primary curriculum.

The books each deal with:

- **coordination**: a role which emphasises harmonising, bringing together, making links, establishing routines and common practice; and,
- **subject leadership**: a role which emphasises: providing information, offering expertise and direction, guiding the development of the subject, and raising standards.

The purpose of the series is to give practical guidance and support to teachers — in particular what to do and how to do it. They each offer help on the production, development and review of policies and schemes of work; the organisation of resources, and developing strategies for improving the management of the subject curriculum.

Each book in the series contains material that subject managers will welcome and find useful in developing their subject expertise and in tackling problems of enthusing and motivating staff.

Each book has five parts:

1 The review and development of the different roles coordinators are asked to play.
2 Updating subject knowledge and subject pedagogical knowledge.
3 Developing and maintaining policies and schemes of work.
4 Monitoring work within the school to enhance the continuity of teaching and progression in pupil's learning.
5 Resources and contacts.

Although written primarily for teachers who are English coordinators for Key Stage 2, Mick Waters' and Tony Martin's book offers practical guidance and ideas for anyone in the school who has a responsibility for the English curriculum including teachers with an overall role in coordinating the Key Stage 2 curriculum and the deputy head and the headteacher.

Whilst making the book easily readable the authors explore the challenge for coordinators within the context of the English National Curriculum and the National Literacy Strategy. They have drawn upon their considerable experience of advising on leadership and language matters, inspecting schools, and running courses. The advice is practical; the aim is high. This book will help readers to develop both the subject expertise they will need and the managerial perspective necessary to enthuse and inform others.

Mike Harrison, Series Editor
May 1998

Introduction

How is the book organised?

The book begins with a summary of the expectations upon coordinators, or subject leaders. These expectations are then addressed through an analysis of the current scene with the emphasis upon literacy strategies at national and school level and the links with the English National Curriculum demands. There is an exploration of the knowledge necessary to coordinate the teaching of English and the 'big ideas' behind speaking and listening, reading and writing within the Key Stage 2 curriculum are explored.

Within each section, aspects of the job of the coordinator are addressed. For instance, 'Getting good things going' as a coordinator includes work on speaking and listening. Similarly, the coordinator job of 'moving policy into practice' uses an example from reading. The essence of the jobs can be inter-changed with the aspects of English; the book is illustrating how the job can be achieved in practice.

The book examines why the coordination of English at Key Stage 2 is such a fascinating yet challenging task. The Teacher Training Agency (TTA) expectations for subject leaders are explored within the context of the English National Curriculum and the national Literacy Strategy. Issues of how to embrace the Literacy Framework and the concept of the

Literacy Hour are addressed within the context of good classroom practice and the overall coordination of the subject.

The book deals with the range of dimensions of the coordinator's job, giving practical examples in English. By using the examples, the techniques and suggestions, and relating them to different aspects of English teaching, you will be able to make sense of a very complicated job and find it fascinating and enjoyable.

Part one The role of the coordinator

Chapter 1   The challenge of coordinating English

Being the coordinator for English at Key Stage 2 is an exciting job. It is also a very daunting one. It is exciting because English is at the root of curriculum success for most pupils. English affects every other curriculum area and the extent to which a child can do well in English will often determine how well the child does in the curriculum as a whole.

To be responsible for English means we have the opportunity to influence the whole curriculum and the whole of children's learning and this makes it exciting. The challenge comes when we realise that to influence the whole curriculum is very difficult and the scale of the task of managing English can be enormous.

As a coordinator for this area of the curriculum, the responsibility of managing successful practice is a positive challenge. To see speaking and listening opportunities growing and developing throughout a school is to see the curriculum come alive. To see children writing in different styles for different purposes, for different curriculum subjects, is to see real purpose in learning within a school. To see children turning naturally to books, finding things out for themselves, studying new areas and getting lost in literature is to see children safely released on their journey through life. To see these things happening is hard work and contains many challenges and the good coordinator will start with a clear picture of what needs to be done.

What needs to be done?

The National Curriculum determines a set of expectations in Key Stage 2 in terms of English. All children are expected to achieve appropriate levels in reading, writing, speaking, listening, and they need success in these key areas. They should have opportunities to develop across a *range* of experiences, they should learn and become competent in a set of *skills*, and they should learn about *standard English and language study.*

What needs to be done can be written in a few lines. The challenge of doing it successfully can take a few years, for behind all these phrases lie enormous complexities.

Some of the complexities

- **There is so little content**
  In most curriculum subjects the content is specified. True, children are expected to learn skills and gain understandings, but in most areas, knowledge and processes are clearly identified and learning activities follow from this. So, in geography children are expected to study certain areas of the world and certain features of the landscape. In history, children are expected to study certain civilisations and periods of British history. In English, there is some specification as to the study of literature and standard English and language study, but for much of the English curriculum there is 'no content'. Because it is content free, it is difficult to organise the learning into clearly defined stages.

- **English is everywhere**
  It is twenty years since the Bullock Report used the phrase 'language across the curriculum'. This report recognised that, if we want children to be effective in their use of English, then English has to be used effectively throughout the curriculum subjects. Therefore, if we are the coordinator for English, we rely on every other subject area to provide the vehicle for the exploration of our subject. Because of

this, maintaining a hold and securing development is difficult, as the subject can be used effectively, or less effectively, or indeed, very ineffectively to promote learning in other areas.

■ **Teachers can do English**

In many areas of the Key Stage 2 curriculum one of the most significant challenges relates to the teacher's lack of subject knowledge and expertise. This tends not to be the case in English. Most teachers can speak and listen, read and write. Most teachers can spell adequately and even their handwriting is passable. Where teachers might struggle with some deeper concepts in mathematics or science, or with their knowledge of history or geography, or their competence in IT, for most, English is an area of security. There will be teachers who have insecurity over minor aspects — apostrophes, punctuation detail, or their 'own difficult' words in spelling — but most teachers feel fairly competent in their own proficiency in English. They might be less certain in the area of literature. Their own reading might not have been extended and their understanding of children's' literature may be slim, but teachers gain confidence from their enjoyment of a few children's classics or favourites and feel safe in the knowledge that they can bring some enthusiasm to bear when using books with children. So, with *Not Now Bernard* or those novels about giant peaches or chocolate factories, they set off confidently to work with the children. The trouble is that many teachers believe that they learned English in certain ways and set out to inflict the same methods upon the children they now teach. Influencing teachers and presenting different ideas, approaches, and opportunities can be a challenge unless the culture of the school is right.

■ **Parent pressure**

Parents want children to do well in English because parents know it is at the heart of the curriculum. From an early stage, parents are keen that their children 'succeed'. One of the problems is that the parents' view of success may differ from the school's and the National Curriculum's views of success. Many parents are more excited by the neatness and presentation of a piece of work than they are by the content.

Many parents are persuaded that their child is reading well by the rate of progress through a series of books rather than the quality of intonation and expression used in reading.

- **Everybody has an opinion**

  Harnessing opinion is difficult in English because nearly everybody thinks they know how it should be taught. It is back to the problem that nearly everybody can do it, so nobody seems to see anybody as an expert. People who can read seem to know how to teach reading; people who can write seem to have a view on how it should be taught. For the coordinator to influence colleagues when they are themselves under the influence of the public debate, can be difficult. Sometimes the coordinator is at this level in their own understanding. So many primary school coordinators are not experts in their subject responsibility. Whoever is charged with developing the subject area needs knowledge of the issues, of the background to the subject, in order to move it forward.

The National Literacy Strategy

In many schools the English coordinator has been 'converted' into the Literacy coordinator in response to the government's plans for raising standards in reading and writing by the year 2002. If this has happened to you, or if you are a newly appointed literacy coordinator, you may have attended the original training programme (in the summer of 1998) with your head and perhaps a literacy governor. The aim of this training was to provide you with advice about the teaching of literacy so that you would be able to lead developments back in your school. Whether or not we agree with every detail of the strategy document we recognise it as an attempt to address some of the complexities discussed above by providing detailed schemes of work (the 'content') and a structure for literacy lessons — the 'literacy hour' (how to teach it). However the key question which must be addressed in school is:

Do the literacy scheme of work and the daily literacy hour equal the English curriculum?

The Literacy Hour and Literacy Scheme of Work	Ongoing Work in English

– Text
– Sentence
– Word
	e.g. Individual reading
	    or
	    Marking children's writing

Blocked Work in English
 	
e.g. Author study
    or
    Set of short stories
	English Across the Curriculum
	
	– Opportunities for children
	– Assessment of children
	    – Speaking and listening for a range of
	      purposes in different groupings
	    – Reading a range of texts
	    – Writing a range of texts

- development of qualities in children...independence, perseverance, collaboration...
- resource implications
- ongoing assessment

FIG 1.1
Principles for teaching English

This is a fundamental question and one which a school must consider as staff discuss ways forward in order to achieve the targets which it has been set in terms of the percentage of children reaching Level 4 in 2002. In discussing the question with coordinators we have found the diagram above useful (Figure 1.1).

The literacy hour and literacy scheme of work

There is no doubting the government's drive to establish an hour a day in every primary school dedicated to the teaching of literacy. There is no point here in going over the ground which will be covered on the training days and in the materials sent out to each school. For the same reason we are not going to explain the recommended scheme of work. From our perspective of offering advice to a coordinator, the key issue is:

How do the literacy hour and scheme of work relate to the other three boxes in our diagram?

In other words which aspects of English are going to be covered in each of the boxes and how will the four cohere as a whole?

Blocked units of work e.g. six weeks devoted to the reading and discussing of a set of short stories of different types (see p. 54) might prove difficult in literacy hours split into 15 minutes/15 minutes/20 minutes/10 minutes. Any English teacher worth her salt would want to read and encourage response to, say, *Spit Nolan* by Bill Naughton for longer than 15 minutes!

Ongoing work such as encouraging and monitoring children's individual reading is unlikely to feature in a literacy hour where the focus is very much on shared and guided reading.

Of course, both of the above imply English time outside the literacy hour, something which schools are definitely going to have to consider.

Across the curriculum children will be reading and writing a range of different texts (e.g. reading history information books and writing imaginary journals of a sailor with Magellan) as well as speaking and listening in different groupings for different purposes.

Perhaps the best way of examining how these aspects of English might link is to take some examples:

1 A blocked unit of work on short stories takes place both within and outside the Literacy Hour. 'English' lessons during which children are read to, or read and respond to, the stories may lead to the opening pages of each story being photocopied and used as the text extracts for the Literacy Hour. These can be considered in detail at the levels of text, sentence and word. Extended writing from some of them, e.g. narrating a third person story in the first person from the viewpoint of one of the characters, could start in the Literacy Hour and then be continued in a further English lesson.

2 The Literacy Hour is used to focus on the generic features of information texts. Children are then explicitly reminded of this work when using their history books in a history lesson.

3 The Literacy Hour is used to focus on journals and their purposes and features, with examples as wide apart as Adrian Mole and Dorothy Wordsworth. This work leads

to a higher quality of historical journals in the history work.

These examples demonstrate how the Literacy Hour can link in a coherent way with the need to provide children with high quality English teaching and the use of English skills in other areas of the curriculum.

In terms of the Literacy Scheme of Work we would suggest that the key exercise will involve comparing and contrasting it with the school's current English scheme plus perhaps a third 'version' such as that produced by QCA (when it was SCAA — this scheme has a speaking and listening strand which is mysteriously absent from the Literacy Strategy scheme). This exercise could be done with reference to the diagram discussed above in order to ensure that the different facets of English teaching are covered.

Finally there is great emphasis in the National Literacy Strategy on developing personal qualities in children so that they are able to work independently, persevere with tasks and collaborate with peers. Certainly we want independent readers, confident writers and children who are involved in their own learning and able to reflect on it.

The discussion and ideas which make up the bulk of this book are concerned with high quality English teaching in its widest sense. Some of them will relate directly to the Literacy Initiative, providing ideas which will ensure high quality literacy hours. Others will raise issues related to the discussion above in terms of where such work 'fits' and how it could link across Literacy/English/other subjects. All of them will contribute to children developing the skills and knowledge necessary for fluent reading and writing as well as developing enthusiasm for these activities and a fascination for the ways in which the English language works.

What is the task?

A 'real' Programme of Study has to be devised by teachers from the statements made in the National Curriculum document and the directions in the Literacy Framework. The school has to decide what the statements mean and build up a rationale for quality practice in English. The 'big ideas' are contained within the National Curriculum text but the reader has to do a lot of reading between the lines in order to fully appreciate what is demanded. The teacher needs to know a lot about the teaching of English in order to fully comprehend the Programme of Study for Key Stage 2.

Given this background, the English coordinator can see the job as four tasks:

- to develop the knowledge of colleagues so that they are clear about why particular approaches represent 'best practice';
- to help colleagues translate the National Curriculum document and the Literacy Framework into 'content' for their classroom teaching;
- to help colleagues to teach well;
- to ensure the development of whole school approaches.

This book will help the coordinator. It is a link between the big ideas in English teaching, the expectations of the Literacy Strategy, and the expectations of the job of the coordinator, which are the same for all subjects. This book relates the job to the subject.

The job of the coordinator relies on an understanding of the subject. Success hinges upon knowing the answer to the question, 'What does quality English teaching look like in the Key Stage 2 classroom?' Knowledge is power. With that power, driving the job forward is easier and the knowledge complements the skills of the job.

Chapter 2 Being a coordinator

So, what is the job?

Subject coordinator, subject manager, person with responsibility for, post holder; all of these are ways that are being used to describe the job of the coordinator. From what were called scale posts of responsibility just a few years ago, primary teachers have moved through various titles towards what is often now called subject manager responsibility. As they have moved through the titles the job has grown and grown, and the expectations upon the person charged with developing a subject in the primary school are large. All the responsibilities usually have to take place around, behind, above and below that central task of running the learning for a class of children.

The Teacher Training Agency has developed a set of standards for different levels within the profession, and within these standards lies a set of expectations for *subject leaders*. The agency sees subject leadership as a key role in the management of primary schools. These key roles are taken by nearly everybody who teaches within the primary sector, for some time ago the Secretary of State insisted that all teachers should take on some subject responsibility and coordination. This means that all subjects have to be divided between all the teachers and in primary schools it never seems to work out

Another book in this series, *Coordinating the curriculum in the smaller primary school*, examines issues concerned with coordinator 'overload'.

as a nice simple equation. Too often there are not enough teachers to go around the subjects and some teachers have to take on more than one. In some cases the teachers take on three, four or five subjects depending on the size of their school.

In other cases the subjects expected do not fit the qualifications and backgrounds of the teachers available, so some teachers end up coordinating and leading subjects in which they have expertise and other teachers take pot luck and some have 'Hobson's choice'. In some schools people are desperate for responsibility and in others responsibility is thrust upon them. Yet if we are all subject leaders, then we are all expected to exhibit the leadership qualities expected by the Teacher Training Agency.

The expectations of subject leaders are clearly spelled out so that national standards can be applied to the knowledge, understanding, skills and attributes of subject leaders within schools. The Teacher Training Agency identifies a *core purpose of* subject leadership and it is useful to think of this within the context of English.

The core purpose of the job is:

 to provide professional leadership for a subject to secure high quality teaching and effective use of resources, and ensure improved standards of achievement for all pupils.

The subject leader is therefore responsible for
■ securing high standards of teaching and learning;
■ raising standards of achievement;
■ supporting, guiding and motivating teachers and other adults;
■ monitoring and setting targets for subject;
■ contributing to policy development within the subject and across the school.

These purposes are the culmination of development over time. Studies such as 'Classroom organisation in primary schools: A discussion paper' (the so called three wise men's survey)

(1992), *Primary Matters* (1994), and successive HMCI Annual Reports, have highlighted the significance of the role of the subject leader and the range of responsibilities undertaken. In good schools subject leaders certainly do these jobs, but in good schools the range of purposes are carefully harnessed and coordinated by senior management in order to help it to work effectively.

The Teacher Training Agency standards for subject leaders highlight *key outcomes of* subject leadership, relating to different partners connected with schools:

- for pupils, there will be improved attainment, knowledge of the purposes of the subject, enthusiasm and motivation, and good attitudes;
- for teachers, there will be teamwork, understanding of the aims of the subject, policies, high expectations of pupils, clear targets, guidance about classroom practice, good use of inspection findings and appropriate teaching approaches;
- for parents, there will be relevant information about the subject and guidance about how they can help their children;
- for senior management, there will be information about the subject to help effective decision making;
- for other adults, there will be information about their roles and ways in which they can be effective.

The outcomes are therefore very much about influencing others, about making a difference, rather than being about provision. The task of the coordinator in English is not just to offer help to colleagues but to ensure that the various partners gain from the work done.

The Teacher Training Agency standards for subject leaders highlight four key areas for development. These are also areas for assessment if subject leaders wish to achieve the National Professional Qualification associated with their job.

The four areas, again, are those which have emerged as significant in the last few years of detailed analysis of success in primary schooling.

1 **Strategic direction and development of the subject**
In this area subject leaders need to develop
  - policies and practices which promote high expectations;
  - staff confidence in teaching the subject;
  - a clear understanding of the importance of English in helping children to grow as people and prepare for adult life;
  - analysis and interpretation of data in order to set targets;
  - planning and resourcing to support the subject;
  - ways to monitor progress and seek further improvement.

2 **Teaching and learning**
Subject leaders are expected to secure and sustain effective teaching and constantly seek improvement through evaluation. They need to ensure
  - coverage, continuity and progression of the subject for all pupils;
  - appropriate teaching methods to achieve objectives;
  - policies and practice for assessment, recording and reporting which enable progress to be made by children;
  - evaluation of the teaching in English and support for teachers in improving the quality;
  - partnership with parents and the wider community to promote effective learning.

3 **Leading and managing staff**
In this area the importance of subject leaders in working with people is highlighted and specific examples would be:
  - set expectations for staff and pupils about the way the subject should be taught;
  - managing new practices;
  - using staff expertise;
  - working effectively with the senior management and other subject leaders;
  - helping teachers to become better at teaching the subject;
  - providing support and training for new staff.

4 **Efficient and effective deployment of staff and resources**
This is one of the oldest responsibilities of those in charge
of any subject and is again emphasised within the job of the
subject leader: to
- establish staffing and resource needs, liaising with senior
  management;
- organise expenditure to meet development plans;
- to create effective and safe working environments;
- ensure good management and organisation of space and
  resources, including IT;
- developing new resources from both within and outside
  the school.

These four areas are significant because they highlight both the
boundaries of the job but also the enormous expectations
placed upon the holder of responsibility. The burden is a big
one to be carried on top of the responsibility for a class of
children that is most teachers' responsibility as well. Although
this has been mentioned before, it is important not to forget
the fact.

If subject leaders are to carry out these jobs with skill, it is
important that they have a high level of subject professional
knowledge. They need to have a detailed knowledge of
effective teaching within their subject and strategies for
improving and sustaining high standards of teaching, learning
and children's achievement. They need to know about the
subject, cross-curricular links and relevant developments,
plus acquiring a broad understanding of the key issues relating
to their own and other subjects. In the context of English this
is an ever-shifting debate that we shall attempt to explore
and offer some positive strategies and approaches that reflect
on the issues and will, hopefully, enhance children's
achievements.

If we are to do this, then it is important to keep up to date
with relevant research and evidence drawn from national
OFSTED inspections. This is explored in the following
pages and attempts are made to show how findings can be
interpreted and used to develop the quality of teaching

offered to children. It is important also that subject leaders have certain knowledge and understanding to help them to sort out the subject and its demands. They need to know how to monitor, develop and improve other people's teaching. They need to understand how the subject relates to other areas. They need to know how children learn and improve, including those with special needs, so that they can consider alternative approaches and outlooks. They also need to know how to interpret the vast array of information that is now finding its way into schools for each subject in order to ascertain exactly what standards the school achieves in relation to the national achievement within the subject. The onus is on the subject leaders to distil information and guidance from documents from the DfEE, OFSTED, QCA and other national bodies in order to help other teachers to interpret the key features quickly, easily and effectively.

Doing all this means an enormous range of *skills and attributes* is needed. The Teacher Training Agency identifies four areas but each contains a list of the features of the super-person who is supposed to do the job.

Subject leaders should be able to:
- lead and manage people;
- solve problems and make decisions;
- communicate with others;
- manage themselves.

The array of skills and attributes is a set of blocks which together form the picture of the job. These blocks are like bricks in the wall to sucess. The wall can either be a barrier or a solid shelter within which people feel comfortable and secure. Holding it all up, the foundation, is the understanding of the subject (see Figure 2.1).

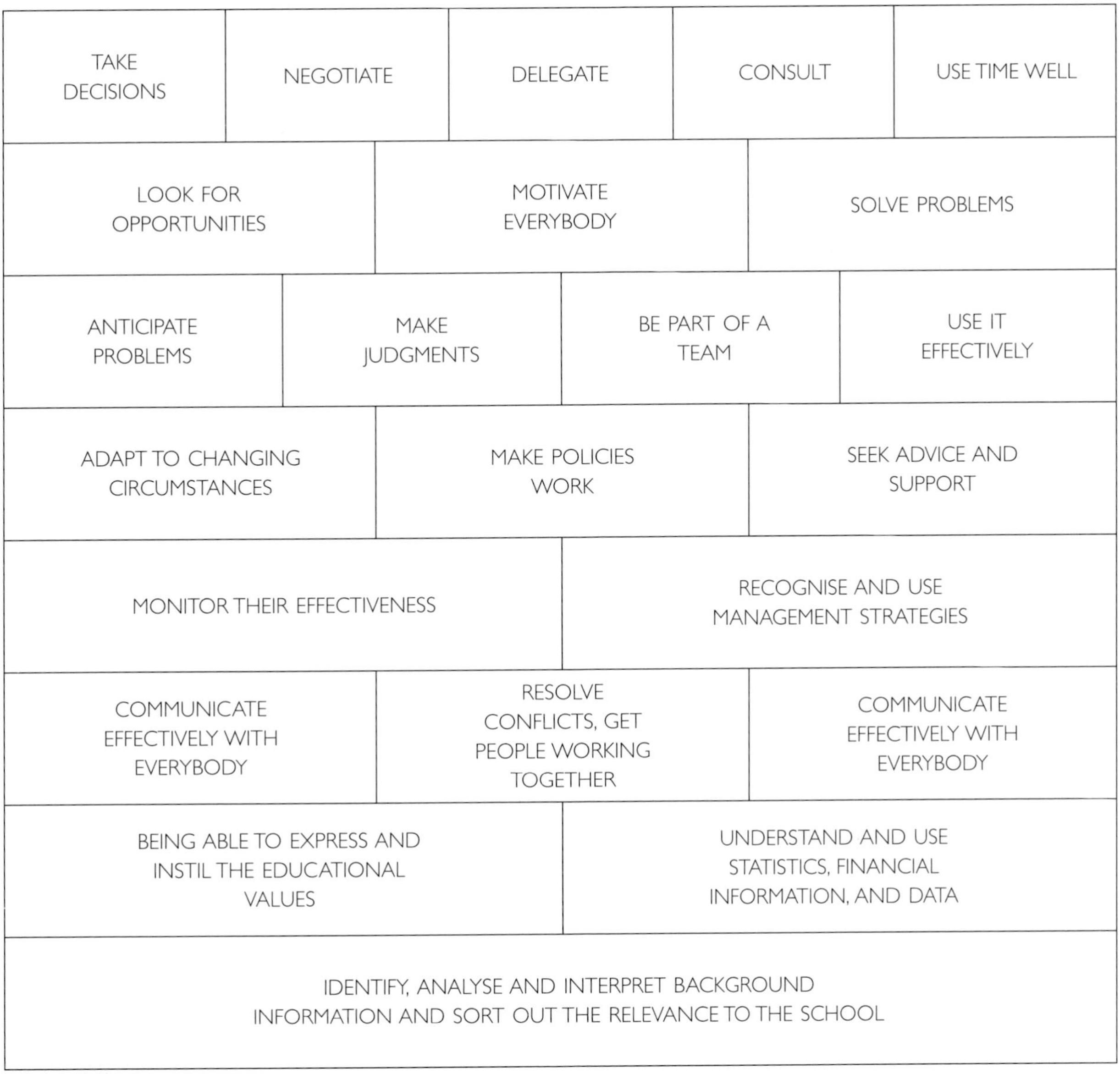

TAKE DECISIONS	NEGOTIATE	DELEGATE	CONSULT	USE TIME WELL
LOOK FOR OPPORTUNITIES		MOTIVATE EVERYBODY	SOLVE PROBLEMS	
ANTICIPATE PROBLEMS	MAKE JUDGMENTS	BE PART OF A TEAM		USE IT EFFECTIVELY
ADAPT TO CHANGING CIRCUMSTANCES		MAKE POLICIES WORK	SEEK ADVICE AND SUPPORT	
MONITOR THEIR EFFECTIVENESS			RECOGNISE AND USE MANAGEMENT STRATEGIES	
COMMUNICATE EFFECTIVELY WITH EVERYBODY	RESOLVE CONFLICTS, GET PEOPLE WORKING TOGETHER		COMMUNICATE EFFECTIVELY WITH EVERYBODY	
BEING ABLE TO EXPRESS AND INSTIL THE EDUCATIONAL VALUES		UNDERSTAND AND USE STATISTICS, FINANCIAL INFORMATION, AND DATA		
IDENTIFY, ANALYSE AND INTERPRET BACKGROUND INFORMATION AND SORT OUT THE RELEVANCE TO THE SCHOOL				

FIG 2.1
Bricks in the wall to success

Starting to influence others

The best place for a coordinator to start is in their own classroom, with their own children, doing the sorts of things that are clearly good practice. Starting to do the things that are good practice within the context of other subjects is even better. If it is possible, teachers should develop the sorts of examples that allow other people to see what they mean by good practice, which creates a real possibility that policy

Some colleagues will not be interested. In which case, it is a matter of looking for somebody else who might want to take on board some good ideas. Good practice can be passed on by opening up the classroom. Simple things like teaching with the door open gives other teachers the chance to come in. One class can write books for other children and take them into another classroom. This makes it very difficult for other teachers not to notice what is going on. If children are taking their work to classrooms, it is worthwhile to plan beforehand a way of reviewing that work so that the other class can comment on it. That means the other class is almost duty-bound and a possibly half-interested teacher may become more interested because of the structured involvement.

Assemblies are a good way to try to get across to other children, and their teachers, the purpose of work. Many children's work assemblies stop short of explaining or underlining the real purpose and the ways in which success has been achieved. People need models and examples to see how things were done. Assembly is not just a chance to show what has been achieved, but a chance to talk about how it was achieved and what conditions were necessary.

guidelines become a reality in the classroom rather than in filing cabinets.

After that, the best place to go is the classroom next door. If teachers can infect colleagues with their enthusiasm, there is the chance to move expertise to other parts of the school community.

It might be useful to offer to help other teachers or coordinators, particularly coordinators who are trying to get their own subject area going. Offering to work in each other's classrooms and working together in geography and English or science and English gives a real chance to link one subject with another. Because English is relevant to every other subject, the English coordinator has every opportunity to help colleagues. One of the problems of showing people things that have been achieved is that it can cause resentment and sometimes it is necessary to show the near-misses, the failures, and the absolute disasters. Some people are more likely to get involved when they realise that their colleagues are struggling and maybe they could offer to help. It is good technique now and again to admit to problems.

Displays of work around the school can encourage discussion with children and their teachers. Again, the display should not be an exhibition of finished work, but ought to offer a picture of how the work was achieved and raise some questions about how it could develop.

There could be invitations in the display for work to develop further elsewhere. Rather than simply focusing on English, the displays might work within other displays: a maths and English display; a history and English display; a writing and reading within the context of science display. These would all give an emphasis to the vehicle for learning, as well as the learning itself. The constant invitation for people to contribute more is well worth developing.

Involving another school can be helpful. Linking with another school and sending them work, perhaps to be reviewed or questioned by children, and receiving back responses and efforts of their children, will not only make an audience and a purpose apparent to children, but will create the opportunity to involve others within the school. When work comes back, it does not have to go directly back to the children who originally sent it, it could go to other children in the school.

The big challenge is to try to impress upon other teachers the need to get involved, so that they are prepared to take those often hesitatant steps that lead them forward into exploring their own teaching and learning techniques.

The job, though, goes beyond this as most teachers will let someone help them with their classroom practice but there is a subtle difference between being allowed to help and taking the lead, establishing strategy, taking the initiative, confronting problems, giving ideas, and establishing policy and checking it is working.

Part two

What the English coordinator needs to know

What you need to know

As the Teacher Training Agency expectations emphasise, to be an effective coordinator it is essential to have a strong grasp of the subject. One of the problems with English is that it gets everywhere! It is such a difficult subject to contain; it appears in every lesson somewhere and the child's success in the curriculum is often limited or supported by the level of success in English. It is a big subject; just look at the average primary school OFSTED inspection report and count the pages devoted to English. Usually, the English section is three times as long as any other subject section. It is a subject that matters and recent government initiatives and legislation demonstrate the general concern for the effectiveness of the teaching of English.

Any book for English coordinators at Key Stage 2 is bound, therefore, to contain a big section on 'what you need to know'. As stated in the introduction, the impression could be that teachers do know about English because they can do it. However, there is far more to it than that and most teachers are only too keen to extend their understanding of the subject.

In this section we consider three key 'big ideas' regarding the teaching of English plus an area which does not appear in the National Literacy Strategy but which has its own Programmes of Study and Level Descriptors in the National Curriculum.

Elsewhere in the book there is much advice offered to coordinators about how to do the rest of the tasks to meet the TTA expectations. We can lead meetings, produce documents, lead INSET, but in the end we are often helping people to get better at something they do not understand. If all teachers were given a copy of this section to consider the key 'big ideas' the task of developing practice would be so much easier because teachers would see the reasons behind the practice they are asked to develop. As a way of helping teachers you might consider providing them with the chance to read this section.

Chapter 3   Working at different levels

Arguably this is the key idea. English is best taught through an examination of how it works in practice, in real texts written for real purposes. Exactly what it is we are teaching can best be considered in terms of the three levels detailed in the National Literacy Strategy:

- **Text level**
  This means learning 'how texts work' in the sense of how they are structured and the 'rules' which operate in them. How does 'narrative' work? What about an information text? Two other key ideas which require careful consideration are how readers respond to and understand texts (comprehension) and how writers use this knowledge to write their own (composition).

- **Sentence level**
  This refers to grammar and punctuation. A major part of the former is concerned with how words work in sentences and the ways in which sentences are constructed. The latter exists because writers need to indicate to readers exactly how what they have written should be read.

- **Word level**
  This refers to phonics, spelling and vocabulary; the ways in which words are constructed and their meanings.

In terms of teaching English at these different levels a powerful model is shown below which reflects the approach of the National Literacy Strategy.

Texts as contexts

1 **Decide on a starting point**
(This could be a text, some reading...a big book, the opening of a novel, a short story, an information book, a newspaper, a poem, a packet or carton, an advertisement, a CDROM...Or it could be some writing actually composed with the teacher by a group or the class.

2 **Consider text level work**
How do we respond to it?...What do we think of it?...What features do texts of this type possess? ...How do we 'read' it?...Why might we read it?...

3 **Consider sentence and/or word level work**
Use the text to investigate whatever it is we want the children to learn. So, the opening page of a novel could be used to
> examine speech punctuation
> trace pronouns through the page
> examine the impact of adjectives or adverbs
> consider words whose meaning is not known
What we do will depend on the children, the text and our teaching objectives.

4 **Decontextualise the learning**
Now we can move beyond seeing a feature of sentences or words in context and can pull it out to examine it on its own. Can we generalise about how speech is punctuated? Can we use the words or techniques in our writing?

5 **Find other contexts showing these features of sentences and words**
Establish an ethos in which children see language as fascinating and are actively involved in noticing it all around them and coming into the classroom to share their discoveries.

6 **Continually refer to the features whenever discussing reading and writing**
There is no point in doing some exciting work on adjectives with examples drawn from poetry, stories, advertising and then not mention the word 'adjective' again for six months.

The teaching of punctuation, grammar and spelling

Our aim is not to come up with detailed ideas for teaching these three vital areas of writing, but to discuss what needs to be established if this teaching is to be successful. Each member of a group of teachers can be given the same lesson plans for a week but may well achieve very different results in terms of successful outcomes. One underlying factor is vital for all of them — establishing in children's minds that they are all fascinating because they show us how the English language works. We must never be afraid of language. It really is one of the most naturally interesting subjects we can study because we all use it all of the time. Our aim is for children to become proficient users of it as listeners, speakers, readers and writers, and they are most likely to do so if they are reflecting on it themselves and then thinking about it and noticing aspects of it outside our classrooms or in their homes and communities.

Punctuation

There is very little written about how children learn to punctuate. As we write, a conference on it has just taken place in Manchester. By the time this book appears we may be in the centre of an explosion of interest in this area!

In terms of the above model for teaching, if the focus is punctuating direct speech we would first find some texts in which speech is being punctuated. From these examples a set of rules could be drawn up which appear to govern its use. These rules can be considered 'out of context' so that children are taking a step back from language in use, having it decontextualised. Then they will try and use it in a suitable text and for a particular purpose, so that their own context is established. We can also search for it in other texts and contexts.

However we must not make the mistake of assuming that we cover it once in a particular week and then expect it to have been learned. As with parts of speech we are dealing with complex issues. How many of us have struggled to explain the use of a full stop to children who appear never to have heard of them or who scatter them like confetti around their work (or place them at the end of each line!). Punctuation is related to sentence structures and while awareness of the latter can be tackled in direct teaching and discussion, we know that it is actually developed through reading. Four-year-olds who have been read stories can dictate stories in suitable sentences. Children develop an ear for written language from their reading — and the wider the range of texts they experience the more sophisticated is that ear. We all know that the children who can string sentences together effectively in their writing are our readers. Because punctuation is allied to something so complex we must continuously 'drip feed' in references to it throughout Key Stage 2, whenever we are discussing a reading text or a piece of writing by a child. A mature understanding of use develops over time as a result of haveing something constantly drawn to our attention. You can explain 'lbw' to a 10-year-old but it will only be fully understood through playing many, many games of cricket.

Grammar

The above model works equally well for grammar teaching. There is no disagreement that it is best approached through a consideration of language in use. In school it could be that there is confusion about why we teach children about grammar at all. This should be addressed by the coordinator in order to clarify aims and objectives in the minds of all staff.

1   We study grammar in its own right because it is our language and therefore worthy of study — in the same way we will be studying literature, for its own sake. Creative ways of doing so, represented in the books we recommend (Chapter 18), should provide all teachers with the confidence to do so as well as catching the imagination of children. Blocked Units of work can be planned with language as their focus. We could be investigating the origins of words and the ways these determine their spelling, or the differences between speech and writing, or the similarities and differences between types of text, or the functions of different parts of speech . . . There is a danger of language always being the backdrop to English work or simply represented by exercises on a particular day of the week rather than a topic for study in its own right.

2   Through studying grammar we provide children with a language which they can use to discuss language. Every subject has its own vocabulary so that in mathematics children learn to use words such as multiply or circle or area. The problem with the language of English is that we only tend to use it in the context of English. Words such as noun or phrase or colon are not generally part of everyday conversation. It follows that if children are not hearing these words used and being encouraged to use them

whenever possible they are unlikely to remember them or even understand them. The key approach in Key Stage 2 is to introduce the terms and then ensure all teachers use them all of the time. In Y3 we are not necessarily expecting the meanings to be clear but if the key words are used consistently over four years we have a better chance of establishing them in children's minds by the end of Y6. Whenever we are discussing or commenting on a child's reading or writing we can use the correct term This is the same 'drip feed' approach as was recommended for punctuation above.

3   We teach grammar in order to improve children's writing. This is actually a tricky proposition with a great deal of research to suggest it is not true which in turn has been questioned by others. We do not see it as a problem in that the above two reasons will ensure children focusing on the ways language works and if such study affects their own writing so much the better. Some of it will go on when children are considering something they have written themselves and so will enable them to step back from their ideas and look at how they have used language. However if children writing in Standard English for different purposes is our goal then the key will be the quality and range of the reading we provide for them. The areas discussed in Chapters 4 and 5 both in terms of managing children's own reading and examining texts in different ways will provide models of written Standard English for their own writing. Look at the examples of the openings of the novels written by Y6 children (p. 00) and consider the lessons that have been learned by the author of Time Travel as opposed to the author of The Mine. Writing is modelled on reading.

Spelling

There are two main ways in which spelling should be taught:

- from children's writing — an individual child's spelling;
- in spelling lessons — working in a pair or in a group.

Our experience suggests that much teaching is not as successful as it could be because it does not aim to get children interested in or actively engaged with words and spelling patterns. It is worth investigating in a school to determine how far children are simply the passive recipients of spellings, whether it be corrections from their writing or lists of words to learn for spelling tests. They may well do the corrections or learn the words in the test but all too often this work does not transfer into further writing (manifest in children asking for spellings which they have already been given!) and is forgotten within a few weeks.

Both of the above aspects of the teaching of spelling should be based on the same three principles:

1 wherever possible a pattern or rule is 'generalised' from a particular word;
2 *children* do the generating of words based on the pattern or rule;
3 the words which are generated are used for further work which will increase vocabulary, focus on the origins of words and lead to a fascination with spelling.

Working from children's writing

When children write we want them to use the best words even if they cannot spell them. A key 'moment that matters to children' in the classroom is the moment when they want to use a particular word in their writing but they are unsure how to spell it. As coordinator this can make a very useful focus for staff discussion

■ Do the same systems apply at this moment in each classroom so that there is continuity of approach?
■ Or do children have to spend the first few weeks of each academic year working out what will apply in the new class?

Our experience suggests that two major systems operate in different classrooms:

1 the children stop writing at this moment and go and find the word. This might involve queuing up with a spelling book in which the teacher will write or going to a word bank or dictionary. Sometimes the word will have been 'tried' initially;
2 the children 'have a go' at the word and carry on writing.

What are we to make of these?

The problem with the first, regardless of what it is that children do, is that it means the writing is being **interrupted**.

For some children it is being constantly interrupted! We make the point in discussing the writing process (p. 181) that the part which we label 'writing' should involve children getting whatever is in their heads down onto paper in the best possible sentences. It is about composing. If, every time a child thinks she needs help on how to spell a word she interrupts herself, there is likely to be a negative impact on the quality of the writing itself. Interruptions interrupt flow. We would add that if the system appears to involve something which the child finds difficult and time consuming (using a dictionary perhaps) or just time consuming (joining the spelling queue) they are likely to use a simpler word which they can already spell. Sometimes we find ourselves trying to assess a child's vocabulary from their writing. In fact we might just be assessing the words which the child thinks she can spell. She may have a much richer vocabulary at her disposal but choose to play safe or take the easy option.

Have a go!

As a general rule, therefore, children should always 'have a go' when they want to use a word they think they cannot spell. However, we would add a number of other considerations if such a strategy is to be most effective:

- Children should indicate that they think their attempt is an error by circling or underlining the word. They themselves much prefer this to just 'having a go'. As a 9-year-old put it, 'If I have a go and it's wrong and I hand my writing in, my teacher will think that I think it's right. But I know it's wrong.' Like any of us, children want it to be known when they realise they have made an error.
- It is fascinating to see how, in the main, even the struggling writers can identify their errors. This means we can turn a negative into a positive. 'Well done, Darren, you have successfully identified all of your 31 spelling mistakes!'
- After they have finished writing children can, either on their own or after discussion with us, find the correct spellings. This is the time for them to use dictionaries, word banks, word books.
- Children do not erase the original error when correcting it. The correction should be written above the word (writing on alternate lines is a useful idea for drafts). We need to see the error in order that we can use it as a potential teaching point. We will decide which word or words have to be followed up by the child.
- From the one error children should not just learn one word, but a whole pattern or spelling rule. When we were at school all

our spellings were corrected and next to some would appear something like 'x 10'. This meant one had to write out the correction ten times. How inefficient! One word might well be learnt but nothing more. Now 'x 10' is that child's **spelling challenge** — to find ten other words with the same pattern or rule. So, if 'crumb' has been spelt 'crum', the correct spelling is discussed or indicated plus another example, say 'limb'. The child now has to find more examples of the same. In actively searching for the words the pattern is held in the child's mind — exactly what competent spellers are able to do.

- Children can test each other on their particular words.
- The word book must not just be alphabetical. We may well want children to put the words they find into an alphabetically organised book for alphabet and dictionary practice. The problem is that because the words may well begin with different letters, they will be put on different pages and the pattern will disappear. They also require a 'spelling book', each page focusing on a pattern or rule. In the above example the page would be headed **–mb**.

Spelling lessons

The same ideas underpin our approach to spelling lessons. Now it is groups of children being set **spelling challenges**, the resulting lists being used for discussion, further work and, of course, learning. This is best approached in ability groups or pairs, though of course whole class sharing of what has been discovered will enable any child to gain from the work of other groups. Basically each group is given a pattern e.g. –gh, thr–, –ea–, or a rule e.g. live/living. The group has to find as many words as possible in, say, three days. A number of things always seem to happen when spelling challenges are introduced:

- Children get very excited about spelling! It is something to do with the word 'challenge'. We all like a challenge. The focus has shifted from 'being tested' to 'contributing' and 'finding out'. Spelling becomes a positive rather than something to worry about.
- Lists of words are produced which are very long! Perhaps a hundred words! Sometimes this is viewed as a problem by teachers in terms of the sheer number and the fact that many of the words' meanings are not known to the children. However there are not really any problems. Firstly, just staring at fifty words containing 'ough' certainly

reinforces the pattern, and this is the aim after all — to imprint the patterns on children's minds. Secondly, new words mean we can move into vocabulary. Children can circle six words they do not recognise, look up their meanings, share them with another group, attempt to use them in some writing, go home and tell their parents. Such work can lead naturally into a fascination with words, their meanings and their derivations — a focus for a Language Unit perhaps.

Examples of spelling challenges

die   sciencetist   untie
lie   Quite   untied
Field remedies   unluckier
Friend rasberries   Auntie
Chief strawberries   Shield
charlie pie
Willie berries   niece
thief   priest   thieves
Quiet   priestess   Handkerchief
premier serviette   fierce
piece   Shabbiest   Filthier
brief   Shabbier   Filthiest
belief Shriek   flies
Mischief Shiniest   funniest
Chillier shinier   glossiest
Sillier entries   gloomiest
fried   tied   galleries
tied   tie   tries
cried   luckier   copies
Science Quietly   cosier
        Quieter   lier

Chapter 4

The reading–writing connection

Throughout this book we stress the interconnections between speaking, listening, reading and writing. We begin this chapter with the same crucial idea. The following are two pieces of writing by two different Y6 children — the opening chapters of 'novels' they wrote in the summer term. Both pieces have been 'corrected' and typed because we do not want to focus at this point on the secretarial features of spelling, punctuation and handwriting — they come later. In reading them two questions need to be asked:

1   Which do you think is the most successful?

2   Why do you think one child is able to write so much better than the other?

Correcting and typing children's work is so useful in enabling us to focus on the content and language. At the levels of **text** and **sentence** what do these children know about writing?

In terms of text, the author of *Time Travel* certainly knows how the openings of stories work. From the opening question which draws us immediately into the story, through the flashback describing the family argument, to the lovely description of the time on the train, we know we are reading something by someone who can write. At the sentence level, the writer is able to use a range of sentence types — simple, compound and complex. Sentence length varies so that the

FIG 4.1
Example of writing: *Time Travel*

TIME TRAVEL

Chapter one

'Why is it always me gets into trouble?'

This thought kept flashing through my head as I packed my case for the second time in 24 hours. Here is how it happened. It was my cousin Liz's birthday party this evening and it was extremely boring. I don't know what came over me but as soon as everyone had arrived I got totally mad and shouted lots of horrible things ending with, 'I hate this stupid party and I hate all of you!'

Liz looked at me funny and I realised my Aunt Nell and Uncle Ian were there and had heard everything. Aunt Nell said to me, 'Well if you hate us that much you can go home instead of staying for the weekend.'

After a long argument I stamped out wondering what my mum would say when Uncle Ian phoned to tell her I was coming home early.

I'm on the train now sitting next to a little old lady in funny clothes beside the window. My face must have looked sad because a wrinkly old conductor looked at me and said, 'It can't be that bad.' I managed a smile for him as I reached inside my jean pocket for my ticket.

'That's better, smiley,' he said.

As he walked away I smiled again at the old lady at the window. She got the message and swapped seats so I could look out of the window. It changes one boring hour into an absolutely fascinating one. I pressed my forehead against the window and put my elbows on my knees. This was my favourite travelling position. Hopefully I will be home soon and I can slide into a nice hot bath before mum gets home from work.

piece 'flows' and direct speech is used sparingly for excellent effect — try reading it aloud to appreciate the techniques which have been used. The piece reads like the opening of a good story — it is certainly extremely successful.

Where has this ability to write come from? What sort of writing lessons has the child undertaken in order to develop this facility with text and language? It is only when we ask such questions that we begin to appreciate the subtlety of what is going on and the power of the reading/writing connection. We see it most obviously in particular words and phrases which have been used: 'I **managed** a smile for him', 'I can **slide** into a nice, hot bath.' There is only one reason for the child's writing

FIG 4.2
Example of writing: *The Mine*

THE MINE

Chapter one

I went to call for Alan and Anthony and Chris.
'Let's go to a mine. Follow me it's just round the bend.'
I went to the next bend, then,
'Let's go in.'
'Alright.'
'Let's go in there.'
'Alright.'

Chapter two

'Can you see what I can see?'
'Yes, come on in.'
'I wonder what that does?'
'Press it and you would get on a seat and fasten your seat belt.'
'Where are we going?'
'To space.'
'Where are we heading to?'
'Mars —'
'How long with each?'
'I don't know. See me pull the lever. We've got to attack.'
'I'm going to fix it.'
'We are getting sucked in. We're going to crash.'
'Where are we?'

ability — we are looking at the work of a reader. Someone who is already an experienced reader of fiction and who is able to model her writing on her reading. At one level she may be well aware of this — perhaps incorporating actual incidents from previous reading or particular techniques such as the flashback or beginning with a question. However while these may have been conscious decisions, the facility with language is unconscious. The child knew nothing of the term 'complex sentence' and was unsure of the meaning of words such as 'adjective' or 'verb'. What readers do is develop an 'ear' for written language, for its flow and patterns. Their writing is based on their reading. (We are not saying that children should not be taught about complex sentences or parts of speech as our comments on grammar p. 28 show, simply that we need to be clear about the reasons for doing so. Investigating how our language works is fascinating, but other forces are at work in the best quality writing produced by our children.)

What then of *The Mine*? Obviously this is a far less successful opening in terms of the features discussed above. After the first introductory sentence we are faced with a piece of writing typical of so many of the stories of our weaker writers. KS2 teachers certainly recognise the almost total reliance on dialogue. If *Time Travel* is modelled on previous reading, what are the models for *The Mine*? Two things seem to be going on here. At the level of text it seems likely that it is modelled on the stories of which the child *has* had wide experience, not from books but from television and film. This means that there is no idea, consciously or unconsciously, of the techniques used by writers to begin stories. On film, the camera can provide in a few seconds what writers have to provide in words and sentences. The setting is there in one shot, the appearance of a character is totally 'described' as soon as she or he appears on the screen. All we hear is dialogue. When we read stories we read so much more. At sentence level, then, the writing is actually speaking, a form of language which the child knows about from their own conversations and what has been heard on screen. The writing of weak writers is due in no small part to their lack of experience of reading. They just do not possess the models in terms of texts, sentences or vocabulary which underpin the best writing by children. As the KS2 coordinator it is important to remember that the quality of writing produced will be a reflection of the quality and sheer amount of reading being undertaken.

Reading/writing information texts

Reading information texts

These two pieces of writing *The Mine* and *Time Travel* are narrative. However, the link between our experience of reading and our ability to write is equally important for children in terms of other texts. A child could not write a successful newspaper article if she had never read one (in fact, read lots of them!).

Studies of the characteristics of information texts have demonstrated their difficulty when compared to narrative. The subject matter is generally not 'people' with whom children can identify and a succession of events which develop momentum, but 'structures' (parts of a flower) or 'processes' (the development of transport). As a result the texts are organised very differently from narrative.

More complex sentence constructions may occur which children will not have met in stories, for example noun phrases made up of a long string of words:

> The remains and shapes of animals and plants buried for millions of years in the earth's rocks are called fossils.

Even the vocabulary may contain pitfalls when words known by the child in terms of their everyday meanings suddenly have new meanings specific to a particular subject:

> A tooth has three *regions*: the *crown* is the part projecting above the gum, the *neck* is embedded in the soft gum and the *root* is out of sight, *anchoring* the tooth in its bony *socket*. Inside the tooth is a fairly hard material which contains some living cells; this is dentine. This dentine cannot withstand wear, so in the crown and neck it is covered with a layer of hard, non-living enamel. The dentine in the root is covered with a substance called *cement*, which helps to fix the tooth in the socket. Inside the socket dentine, in the centre of the tooth, is a hollow pulp cavity containing nerves, a small artery and a small vein.

In the past few years there has been a concerted attempt by publishers to provide information texts for younger children in KS1. There has also been advice on how to use them in order to begin the process of familiarising children with their characteristics before they encounter them further up the primary school. Just as children develop 'an ear' for the rhythms and structures of narrative from the stories they hear, so they need to recognise the characteristics of other genres.

It must not be forgotten that exactly the same problems occur with computer generated texts such as CD ROM. These could well signal the end of the traditional information book in that they can provide so much more; not only photographs, pictures and diagrams of equal quality but sound, moving pictures and video. Far more information can be stored on a disc than any one book. However in the end it is the text which counts and the very same issues described above apply equally to CD ROM. As adults we can quickly be seduced by the technology (children seem to take it much more for granted!) and not look too critically at the difficulties posed for children.

The only way to overcome the potential problem of text difficulty is through children reading and using these materials regularly. The greater the experience of them the easier they become to use. There are few if any short cuts. The amount of sustained reading some children do in a typical week can be incredibly small. Yet sustained reading of different texts is the key to being able to being able to use them effectively. In this instance we really do learn to read by reading. Further ideas are discussed in Chapter 7.

The difficulties children encounter trying to make their way through information texts and comprehend what they are reading lead to the second potential problem:

Being able to chose relevant details

This will depend on both the purpose for reading and the type of passage being read. A child might be searching for a precise piece of information (the date the Second World War began) or trying to learn about something wider (the reasons for the war taking place). The dangers of children not really understanding what they are reading and then producing their own writing which they still do not understand, are well known! Sometimes the child has simply copied. The example of the struggling 10-year-old who had spent many hours copying pages from a book on the solar system which he could not read, is a vivid memory. When asked if he understood what he had written, he replied, 'No. It's Topic.' The way he said it clearly indicated that in his mind Topic had nothing to do with understanding, but was about producing some writing and pictures which looked like he had worked hard for the required period of time. The CD ROM topic, much easier than copying because one can colour print text and pictures, is already making an appearance!

Of course, these problems are less likely to occur if children are involved in work with a definite aim in mind. Still though, the ability to translate information into their own words and to note that information for future use in a display or exhibition or booklet, is a challenging skill to be developed. In KS2 the most useful strategy to establish in school is that of children using **models** which, if necessary, can then be used themselves as the basis of writing if it is required. A model is simply a representation of a passage in picture or diagrammatic form. To move straight from text in the book to their own text, with pictures or diagrams drawn afterwards as illustrations, is difficult for young children. To draw first (even if it is a picture copied from the book) means the child now has something other than the book's text from which to construct their own writing. The book can be closed and the drawing or diagram translated into the child's own words.

Models are an aid to comprehension, trying to construct one forcing children to grapple with the meaning of a text. However, having done so we would want them to develop their ability to produce their own information writing. This is the third potential problem:

Writing information fluently and coherently

Here is an extreme example from a 9-year-old child where his ability to compose narrative contrasts strongly with the almost tortured prose he constructs when writing for information. The typed pieces have been corrected in terms of spelling, punctuation and layout so that we can focus on the content and use of language. The original 'Marabou Stork' has also been included (see Figures 4.3 and 4.4).

In the story, the child displays a knowledge of how narrative works. It reads like a written story. Of course he has an even stronger model here — the original novel *Mrs. Frisby and the Rats of Nimh* on which to base his writing. 'The Marabou Stork' shows him trying to explain something he has learnt. The second sentence is interesting as he appears to begin it, 'One of the toes . . .' and then decides he needs to be more specific, '. . . on the left toe'. The word toe is repeated three times and to an experienced reader the effect is clumsy and poorly written. But, of course, an inexperienced reader would not recognise the problem. If the child does not know how information writing should sound he has no model of language on which to base his own efforts.

This might appear to be simply a 'writing' issue best dealt with elsewhere. However, as is stressed throughout this book,

FIG 4.3
Example of narrative and prose.

The Marabou Stork   Sept '92

The stork has a fin foot with three toes and sharp nail and lines down its toes. One of the toes, on the left toe there is one strip going down his toe. On one of his toe has no strips on his foot.

The Marabou stork has a red lump on its neck and a ?. Its beak is his nose with green lumps all over this nose.

Mrs Frisby and The Rats of Nimh   Late November '92

Mrs Frisby went to Nicodemus for help. She knocked on the door and there was a guard called Brutus. He sent her away. She went into the woods and she saw Mr Ages in the woods so Mr Ages took her back to Nicodemus.

He had finished the meeting and took her into the library and she explained about Timothy, about what was wrong with Timothy.

'Can you help me?'
'Yes, I think I can help you Mrs Frisby. I will get all of my men and help you move house.'
'Thank you Nicodemus.'
'I will see you soon, Mrs Frisby.'

The next day Mrs Frisby went back to Nicodemus. She knocked on the door. The door opened.

'Hello Mrs Frisby' said Justin, 'Come in.'
'Where is Nicodemus?'
'He will be coming soon'.
'There he is Justin'
'Hello Nicodemus, do you have a plan yet?'
'Yes, here is the plan. We will get all my men and we will disconnect the lift and get Timothy and bring him here. But just remember the slightest bit of cold will kill him.'

the separating of 'reading' and 'writing' gives a misleading impression of how children learn to read and write. The ability of a child to write well in a particular genre, be it narrative, information or whatever, stems directly from the reading which the child has experienced — what has been read to them as well as what they have read themselves. If we want children who can write in a range of different ways then they need to be reading the same range. Improving the ability of the boy who wrote the above will mean reading lessons as much as writing lessons — in fact literacy lessons. Here we want to stress how much he requires to read the texts we want him to be able to write: to have them modelled in paired and group reading sessions and to take them home as 'reading books'.

FIG 4.4
The original 'Marabou Stork'.

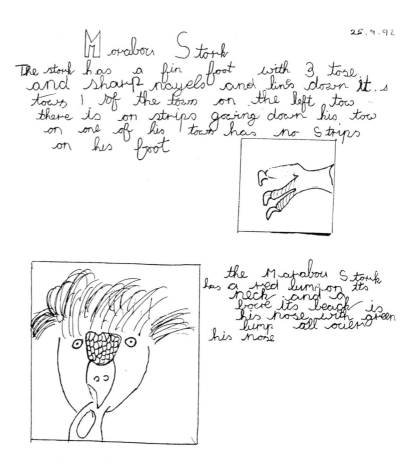

25.9.92

Marabou Stork
The stork has a fin foot with 3 tose
and sharp nayels and lins down it.s
tows 1 of the tows on the left tow
there is on strips going down his tow
on one of his tow has no strips
on his foot

the Marabou Stork
has a red lump on its
neck and on
boove its beack is
his nose with green
lump all over
his nose

While we have stressed experience of reading different types of text in order to develop the 'inner voice' necessary to compose them, two further points need making. Firstly, this issue becomes a key area when considering shared and guided reading at Key Stage 2. In the former, complex sentences (especially long, complex sentences) are read aloud in context by the teacher. These can then be considered explicitly in terms of drawing attention to the intonation required to read them. Children can then join in the reading and discuss how the sentence needed to be read. Similarly, following silent, guided reading when the teacher is discussing and asking questions, individual children can be asked to read relevant sentences and attention can be drawn again to intonation.

Secondly, writing frames can be developed which offer children sentence level support through the provision of sentence openings ('The first point to consider . . . However . . . In addition . . . Therefore . . .') and a structure for the text being composed. Different frames are used for different types of writing and can be constructed with children in shared and guided writing (Examples of books focusing on writing frames are included at the end of the book in the list of resources for teachers). So, regular experience of reading, with reading intonation explicitly modelled and discussed, plus the use of writing frames, aim to develop the 'inner voice' at sentence level. This is a key feature of literary competence and equally important when teaching the reading and writing of any type of text.

Responding to children's writing

In addition to learning about writing from their reading, children will also learn from us if we approach the task of responding to their writing as a teaching strategy. As coordinator you may well have been involved with the development of the school's marking policy. In some schools this is simply agreement on a set of editing symbols which all teachers will use and there is little consideration of the principles which might underlie how we mark children's work. There is also the area of responding orally to writing — most children experience having teachers comment on or ask questions about their work both orally in the classroom and writing when it has been 'marked' at home or in the staff room. In this section we want to address some of the key underlying ideas which ought to be considered if we want to use this process to its full potential as a chance to **teach** a child something about writing or being a writer. We must not lose sight of the major aim of this as a teaching tool — so that the child will learn from it and become a 'better' writer next time. If no progress is apparent from one piece to the next in terms of what was drawn to the child's attention, we do have to stop and consider critically what we are doing.

Involve the child — children as thinkers as well as doers

We have a vision of a Y6 child approaching us with a piece of writing (either finished or unfinished) and beginning to speak. 'I've decided to do it this way because . . . but I'm having a bit of a problem with this bit. I'm quite pleased with this next bit, especially this sentence . . . but I can't think of a really good word for explaining this. I'm not sure how to spell 'scientist' I've had a go but it doesn't look right. Can you help me with the speech marks here?' A familiar scenario in the classrooms in your school? If so you are well on the way to helping children really learn from their own work — because they are thinking about it rather than just doing it. If not, it is worth considering the danger of children doing writing for us and then handing it over to us to do all the thinking about it. Establishing an expectation that children talk to us about their writing before we offer our help should not be too difficult if it is approached with staff in terms of developing children as **thinkers**. After all, surely that is what we are all aiming at? In practical terms its establishment can be approached through:

> The use of open questions at the beginning of conversations with children about their work (of course these questions can be written if we are looking at writing away from the child — with the expectation that the child will respond in writing to them). Such as
> - Can you tell me about this piece of writing?
> - Which parts are you pleased with? Why?
> - Is there anything you think you could improve?
> - Why did you start/organise/finish the piece like this?
>
> Consideration with children of what might be on an agenda for considering a piece of writing. This could form the basis of a poster on display in the classroom 'When I discuss my writing with someone I could discuss . . .' Features appearing on such a poster should cover
>
> The content (What is it about?)
> The process (Why did I approach it like this?)
> The editing (Is it correct?)
> The evaluation (Is it any good?)

Look for specifics

While we want children to **initiate discussion** of their writing we want to use each piece as a **teaching opportunity** to move a child on as a writer. In so doing we will be focusing on at least one aspect of their writing. There is a danger of us making generalised, positive comments ('Well done.' 'A really good story.' 'Well written.') but the only specifics to which we draw a child's attention are those which are incorrect or we feel are unsatisfactory. We imagine a child telling a friend that teacher had written 'A really good story.' after her work. The friend asks, 'What's good about it?' and the child is unable to answer. Children learn as much from what they have done well as from what is not so good. Therefore we need to be pointing out some specifics which are good — after all if it was a good story we must have some idea why we made the comment!

Link response to purpose/teaching points

This simply means letting children know *before* they begin a piece of writing what the criteria will be for success. This could be linked to purpose — what is the purpose of this report/account/story . . . ? What features will make it successful? In this way children will themselves be focusing on the features as they plan and write. Such an approach can also be linked to particular aspects of grammar or punctuation — following work on punctuating direct speech, one key feature of a story involving a family argument will be how successfully children have applied what they have been learning. Work on adverbs might lead to poems in which the adverbs used will be a key focus for consideration. Spelling will always figure as discussed in Chapter 3.

Don't be afraid to criticise

By this we mean being critical of more than just the secretarial skills of spelling, punctuation and handwriting. Perhaps we are too happy to accept what children have produced especially if we know they have worked hard on it. However, the aim ought to be the establishment of an ethos in which everyone knows that all writing can be improved. Children should expect us to value and celebrate their efforts but also know that we will be pointing out areas which might have been better . . . 'I'm not sure I think that sentence works there . . . Try and think of a more effective word here . . . What do you reckon to this sentence? . . . Have you ever heard of this word? . . . In art or technology we see it as vital that we improve the techniques of children, intervening to show the effects that can be achieved by particular shading or combination of materials. The same needs to apply to English if we want children to make the maximum progress.

Chapter 5   The range of reading

In adult life we read a range of different texts for different purposes and, in so doing, build up a knowledge of the ways in which each of them works. We use this knowledge every time we are faced with something to read and it is a major factor in our ability to comprehend what we are reading. The term **literary competence** means knowing the 'rules' which apply to different types of reading, and its development in children is a major objective of the Key Stage 2 curriculum. Anyone reading this book will have the literary competence to read say, a newspaper or a poem or a novel. Presented with a poem we all switch to 'poem mode' and read it in an appropriate way. We would not read a newspaper in the same way. Because we are such experienced readers we tend to use our literary competence without even being aware we are doing so — it takes a totally new type of text to make us consider explicitly our need to know the rules.

There is a danger that we make assumptions regarding what children know about how texts work. At a surface level we recognise that they need to learn that an information book will have a contents page and index but their ability to read, comprehend and use such a book will depend on much more subtle features from page layout to the way sentences, paragraphs and sections are actually constructed.
Consider a simple text found on a card in a newsagent's window:

> BRIGHT & SPAC. ONE DBLE BED FST FL APART

You will have read this without difficulty but only because you are aware of the conventions which apply to it. It only makes sense if you read it with this knowledge in mind. Other texts, for example poems, may have much more complex conventions.

We build up literary competence through reading. There is certainly work which we can do in the classroom in this area, and this is discussed below, but children who read widely will be developing their knowledge with every text. Each novel a child reads helps that child read the next novel — without necessarily any explicit realisation of what has been learned.

The National Curriculum states

 Pupils' reading should be developed through the use of progressively more challenging and demanding texts.

It would be equally true to say that pupils' reading **will** be developed through their **reading** of progressively more challenging and demanding texts, hence our need to provide a range of different types of reading material in our schools and classrooms. The National Curriculum rightly emphasises this point.

There is one potential problem with the use of the word 'range'. While we may be ensuring different types of book and other reading materials are in our classrooms, we can find ourselves providing opportunities to read far more of some types of text than others. Perhaps a better way of approaching it is to think of a reading 'diet'. In terms of food, the aim is a balanced diet and it is just the same for reading at Key Stage 2. It is interesting to determine just what sort of a diet the children in your school are being offered. The danger with notions of range is that it might mean particular types of reading material dominate while others only appear once or twice in a school year. So we might do some work on newspapers only in the Spring term in Y5 but the children are

My reading diet

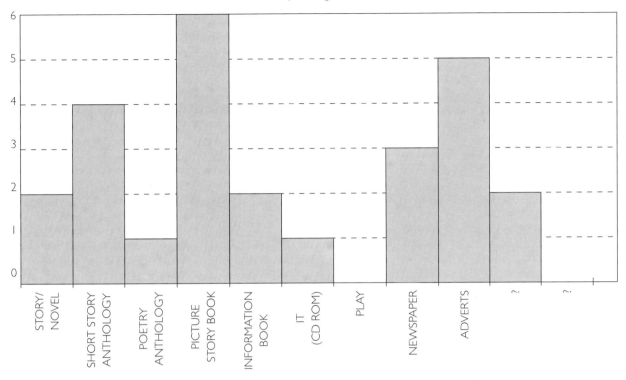

FIG 5.1
Reading diet graph

reading stories/novels week after week. We have then covered a 'range' as required by the National Curriculum, but a somewhat unbalanced range. Traditionally, children have read a great deal of narrative but not much, at any length, of anything else. This results in a skewed reading curriculum represented in Figure 5.1 above.

A balanced reading diet would not be dominated by any one form of reading and this graph can be used by children to keep a record of their own reading. It also has a more powerful use in that it will give both children and their parents important messages about what we mean by reading. What we are suggesting is that this graph should represent the **reading books** which children are helped to choose.

Traditionally children's reading books have been almost exclusively narrative. The older schemes are based around stories, even those which continue into Key Stage 2. The texts might have been longer and more complex than those for

Key Stage 1 but they were still stories. Even when children were allowed to progress to being 'free readers' this meant moving from scheme stories to novels. A child's 'reading book' was a story — other types of reading were encountered to a greater or lesser extent in the classroom but were not designated as 'reading books'. More recent schemes have recognised this problem and at each 'level' provide stories, poetry anthologies, plays and information books. However, we do not need schemes in the Key Stage 2 classroom if our aim is children's reading being a balanced diet.

The use of schemes at Key Stage 2 needs consideration here, as for some children they will be responsible for providing the 'range' required in the National Curriculum. What part should they play in the reading of 8, 9 and 10-year-olds? In our view there is a great danger of schools wasting hundreds of pounds on colourful, tempting new books when the range can actually be far better covered through the books already on the shelves supplemented by reading materials brought into school from outside. A child who is capable of reading *The Iron Man* (Ted Hughes) or *A Necklace of Raindrops* (Joan Aiken) ought to be reading them, not being prevented from doing so by having to read books at Level 29 on a scheme.

Before any decisions are taken which involve spending money an audit needs to be carried out of exactly what is already in school. If stocks are looking somewhat tired and in need of replacement we must beware of choosing the 'easy' option of the scheme rather than investing in the very best of children's books with the help of a children's librarian. And surely we want our children to have access to the very best?

Narrative and poetry — literature at Key Stage 2

Within the range of reading we will now consider two important types of text: narrative (stories and novels) and poetry. A clear rationale will be established for approaching them in the classroom together with ideas for teaching. The reading of **information books** was considered in Chapter 4 (p. 37).

The key word in a rationale for approaches to literature in the classroom is 'response'. Whenever we read or listen to a story or a poem (or watch a play or a film) we respond — we feel and we are made to think. Response is the same whether it is a 4-year-old listening, wide-eyed, to *Little Red Riding Hood* or a 44-year-old reading an adult novel. Exploring with children how they respond to what they read is the basis for classroom discussion and through such discussion we can focus on aspects of reading that we want to teach. Reading is, in fact, generally a solitary activity for adults. In classrooms children can experience a text together so that it becomes something social to be discussed (perhaps the nearest adult equivalents are the reviews of books in newspapers and journals). But think of a group of adults who have gone as a party to the cinema or theatre. Afterwards in the pub or car or coach, they will be discussing what they have seen: 'Oh, it did make me laugh!'; 'I loved the scene when . . .'; 'Wasn't the ending a shock?'; 'I know just how the father felt.' Such comments indicate powerful responses and we all love talking in such ways. If we watch something on television, alone, which moves us, we cannot wait to get to the staffroom next morning to see if anyone else watched it and to tell someone, who did not, all about it!

There is no doubt that beginning with personal response is the most effective teaching strategy for fiction and poetry at Key Stage 2. As a coordinator you need to provide teachers with ideas for exploring response in the classroom, indicating the teaching points which can be developed from such lessons. Unfortunately in the National Literacy Strategy the word 'response' does not appear in the detailed discussion of the Literacy Hour. This could be because the word 'comprehension' (which is used) is felt to focus attention more rigorously on what children are learning from texts, while 'response' may be viewed as little more than children's likes and dislikes. As we shall see below nothing could be further from the truth in terms of a true appreciation of what is meant by 'reader-response'. Indeed if comprehension is viewed as an active engagement with a text we are unsure of the difference between the two words. Let us hope this is the reasoning behind the mysterious omission of response to literature from a framework for teaching reading and writing.

Defining response — what happens when we read?

So, what do we mean by 'response'? The question which needs to be asked on an inservice session is:

If you are someone who reads fiction (be it Jane Austen or Mills and Boon) why? If you are not someone for whom the reading of fiction is particularly important, why do you think others do?

We guarrantee you will always get the same answers: escapism, relaxation, enjoyment...

A nice point to make is that if these words are the hooks which catch many adults, then surely they will be the hooks to catch children. Therefore in our classrooms and teaching...

The next stage is to explain that actually these words are not much help! We all 'enjoy' lots of activities, from eating good food to listening to music, and notions of enjoyment vary tremendously. Just what does enjoyment mean when we refer to reading fiction?

When teachers discuss these words in depth they find themselves discussing some fascinating areas. A flip chart can be used to list them. For example:

- Readers make connections between their own lives and the 'lives' of the characters in the story — 'I've been there'; 'I've felt like that'.

- At times the power of the reading is such that readers feel they are almost living the story themselves.

- Readers 'identify' with particular characters, who are sometimes nothing like them.

- Readers turn the text into pictures in their minds, so that they can 'see' places and people. Scenes are viewed from particular stand points so that readers can often describe 'where they were' at a particular moment in the action.

- Readers predict their way through stories. But not just in the sense of wondering what will happen next, more because they want certain outcomes and definitely do not want others.

■ An 'enjoyable' reading experience may make us feel very sad or frightened or shocked — emotions one would think we would want to avoid.

Response is all about these and other fascinating areas of the reading process. A simple model is that there are two 'sides' to the reading process: a reader and a text.

Reader ⟷ Interaction ⟷ Text

As we read, the text certainly acts on the reader but we must not forget that the reader also acts on the text. Reading is not a passive process — readers do a great deal of the work! We bring ourselves to whatever we read, so that the text comes out to us and we go into the text. The list above of aspects of reading to which adults refer when they analyse what 'enjoyment' means are very much on the 'reader' side of the process.

Where reader and text meet there is an **interaction** — and it is this interaction which accounts for our response. Traditionally right through school and into university the focus has been on only one side of the process — the text, thereby ignoring the reader's responses as listed above. Whether it has been questions which ask 5-year-olds what they can remember about a story, or those which want an undergraduate to describe the character of Silas Marner, readers have been faced with text-based considerations. The reader has been forgotten. We certainly want children to learn about how texts work but the best way into such work is through their own personal responses. Ask 5-year-olds to talk in pairs about the 'best bit' of a story and how it made them feel, and they will certainly do so! Part of the reason is that there are no right or wrong answers — if a child thinks a particular part is the 'best bit' then so be it. As newspaper critics demonstrate every week when reviewing books, plays, films, records, there is no one right opinion — if there was, all of them would write nearly identical reviews. Where one critic sees a great new novel, another dismisses it as worthless. In Key Stage 2 once children have been encouraged to discuss and express feelings and views we can use these to draw attention to how the text works.

Discussions with staff of the above ideas lead to the question of how to approach them in the classroom. We need to work at investigating short stories and novels and below we describe key activities for such work. As coordinator a key strategy may be to go in and lead a lesson along the lines described below. Alternatively help can be offered for teachers planning such work.

While the focus is on short stories, all of the work described below is equally valid for novels in the classroom and is easily adapted for use in the key activities described in the 'Range' section — paired reading, group reading and teacher reading aloud to the class. Such activities support children who may not have developed 'reading stamina' and who are still outfaced at the thought of attempting to read over one hundred pages of small print (with very few pictures!). While short stories are worth reading in their own right, they can also draw children who require such extra support into narrative. The sorts of teaching which can be planned and the insights children gain will be taken to the longer narratives we want them to be able to read for themselves.

Using short stories

Working on a set of short stories over a number of weeks enables us to focus on aspects of narrative in a Blocked Unit of English. We are able to choose stories which vary in terms of subject matter, style and structure. This will mean children are presented with a range of short stories each of which will increase their literary competence to read further stories for themselves.

Subject matter — stories with a **range of settings** — historically, geographically and culturally — some which children can readily identify with in terms of their own lives and some which take children into places and times far removed from their own. They should vary in terms of **the effect** they are aiming at having on the reader — making us laugh, cry, excited, shocked. Some should have strong story lines so that the **plot** is the main attraction. Some should have **underlying themes**, so that perhaps there is very little plot but an exploration of **character** or **situation**.

Style — the stories should vary in terms of **the writer's style**. Some stories contain a great deal of **dialogue**, others a lot of **description**. There are stories written in the **first person** with a **narrator** who is one of the characters while others are written in the **third person**. Some of the latter have **a clear 'voice' narrating**, and perhaps even commenting on, the story. In others we are hardly aware of the narrator. The **vocabulary** may be instantly accessible to the children or it may contain words and phrases (perhaps historical) which will require discussion. There may be an attempt to use non-standard dialect in the conversations.

Structure — some stories are clearly focused around one **major incident** which lies at its heart. Others build up to a **climactic ending**. The **opening paragraphs** can vary widely. In some a character or a place or an object is clearly established before the plot begins. Others start with something dramatic so that the reader is caught up in action very quickly. The **ending** may tie up all the loose ends so that the story very obviously has finished while another ending may be more open with the reader invited to speculate about what it means or what might happen now to a character.

Exactly how we might use the stories in the classroom will, of course, vary depending on the story. However we would suggest some key elements in the approach to such work.

Teacher reads aloud

One of the key aims of working with children on a range of short stories is to enable them to go and read further stories for themselves. Most of the stories ought to be challenging for children on the basis of teaching being about working with children just beyond where they could work unaided. Our reading of the story — our use of varied intonation, rhythm and pace — will enable the children to respond to and comprehend a text they might find too difficult to read alone. This means we can use any story with the whole of a mixed ability class. In addition our reading will demonstrate to children just how such a story ought to be read. We will be modelling reading for them. Further stories can be read as a group reading exercise or taken away by children to read alone.

Stories can be discussed

Discussion before reading — exploring expectations
Before any reader, adult or child, starts to read a short story they will have expectations. It is important to explore these in the classroom before we read any of the key short stories in a Blocked Unit. In fours, each group with a large sheet of paper and a pen (and agreement as to who will be scribe!), children can list their expectations. So, the story is called 'A Necklace of Raindrops', the author is Joan Aiken and it is ten pages long — what are your expectations? There are three main categories of expectation:

1   The title — there is liable to be a necklace of raindrops in the story . . . it sounds like a fantasy . . .
2   The author — I've already read or heard other stories by Joan Aiken so I think there will be magic in it . . . it will be exciting . . .
3   The reader — I think short stories are boring so I won't enjoy it . . . I love listening to short stories . . .

Expectations can be gathered on to a class list and attention drawn to where they came from. Then they need hiding until the story has been read, when they can be a fascinating focus for further discussion — did the story match our expectations?

Discussion at the end
Some times a story can be read right through without any breaks in order for its power to affect the children. Indeed there are stories which will be ruined if constantly interrupted for discussion. We want them to draw the children into what Tolkein called the 'secondary world' which the author has created. As we read the final words and (if the magic has worked) we find ourselves faced with one of those powerful reading moments in the classroom full of held breath and fierce concentration. What should we do now? We must not forget that our aim at this point is to manage some teaching not to treat the exercise as some sort of assessment. We want children to learn from the experience and to contribute to that learning, and the best way of doing this is to encourage and manage discussion. So, we have a choice of three options:

1 Ask some questions — There is a danger that this can kill discussion rather than encourage it, unless the question really does invite genuine response. The sort of question geared to testing memory (What did the North Wind first say to Laura?) or comprehension (Why did Meg steal the necklace?) will involve some children, but we would argue that such questions are not useful as discussion prompts. Their place is later (though quite what place memory questions have in terms of how readers read stories we are not sure!).

2 Look back at the expectations — children discuss in their fours and then we manage a class discussion.

3 Share our enthusiasm — we must never be afraid to allow a few moments silence at the end of a powerful short story. Then we can say what *we* think and/or feel. 'Well, what an ending . . . , What a story . . . I really liked the bit when . . . I never thought for a moment that she would . . .' What we are providing is a role model in terms of someone who genuinely enjoys reading and who also enjoys sharing their response. Such an approach can lead to children in pairs or small groups discussing parts of the story which they particularly enjoyed.

The reading of stories can be investigated

The aim then, as a starting point for further work, is simply to get children discussing enthusiastically. Now we can use this enthusiasm to investigate aspects of **the reader's response** and **how the text has worked**. In terms of the **reader** we can focus on any of the features of the reading process described above in the discussion of 'response':

■ readers make connections between their own lives and the 'lives' of the characters in the story — 'I've been there'; 'I've felt like that';

■ at times the power of the reading is such that readers feel they are almost living the story themselves;

■ readers 'identify' with particular characters, who are sometimes nothing like them;

- readers turn the text into pictures in their minds, so that they can 'see' places and people. (Scenes are viewed from particular stand points so that readers can often describe 'where they were' at a particular moment in the action.);

- readers predict their way through stories (But not just in the sense of wondering what will happen next, more because they want certain outcomes and definitely do not want others.);

- an 'enjoyable' reading experience may make us feel very sad or frightened or shocked — emotions one would think we would want to avoid.

Any one of these areas make for fascinating discussions for children in pairs or small groups. Ideas and feelings can be shared and then pooled for the whole class to consider.

In terms of **the text**, depending on the story, we could focus on any of the features of stories listed above under the headings **subject matter**, **style** and **structure** (p. 54). The aim here is not to introduce some watered down lit. crit. exercises into the primary school but to begin to show children the range of stories that have been written and the ways in which writers construct them. So the opening paragraphs of each story can be photocopied and compared — Which do the children think is the best? Which is the worst? How do they differ? Could we re-write the worst in order to make it better? The important point to bear in mind is that such work should not interfere with the powerful responses which can be generated when the story is first read. Further investigation can be left to another day.

Openings of novels

Another way of focusing children on narrative texts is to investigate the openings of novels, using the response ideas described above. Children can discuss them in groups or even be faced with a copy of the opening page and the chance to actually mark the text.

In the first example Somia and Sabina (Y3), for whom English is a second language, have been asked to indicate the words

Examples of investigating the opening of novels

Y3

1. Discovery in a chalk-pit

'What's going on?'
'Something exciting!'
'Where?'
'Down at the old quarry.' — *Don't understand.*

don't understand.

The news flashed through the village and shopkeepers locked up their shops and ran. Housewives rushed out of their houses without even bothering to bolt the doors.

don't understand

Jed Watkins raced along – as usual, well behind the other boys – down the narrow, muddy, rutted lane leading to the disused chalk-pit. He could smell wood burning. Whatever could have happened? It was at a time like this that he wished he wasn't so much smaller than other boys of his age. He couldn't run as fast and he was always last on the scene.

don't understand — *don't understand*

When, panting, he arrived at the pit, most of the villagers were already there and two

Jed has blonde hair and a J on his T-shirt and a blue Pantan and black shose. Pant's and black shoes.

The old quarry has stons and brick's on it.

The boy's have some orange shoes on. And some shorts and some trx some hats on some bag's with them. Pockes The pock ets were on the bags.

The village has people in it and shop's in it.

The shop keers have some aprons some aporon's on and some glofx gdophs on.

The horse wives look like this they have blond hair and a red dreess dress ohr on and blakk black teits ohr on and red shoes oh. on on.

In the news-flash there was a man which which whith greyish hair and a blue jumper and black Pant's and black shoes.

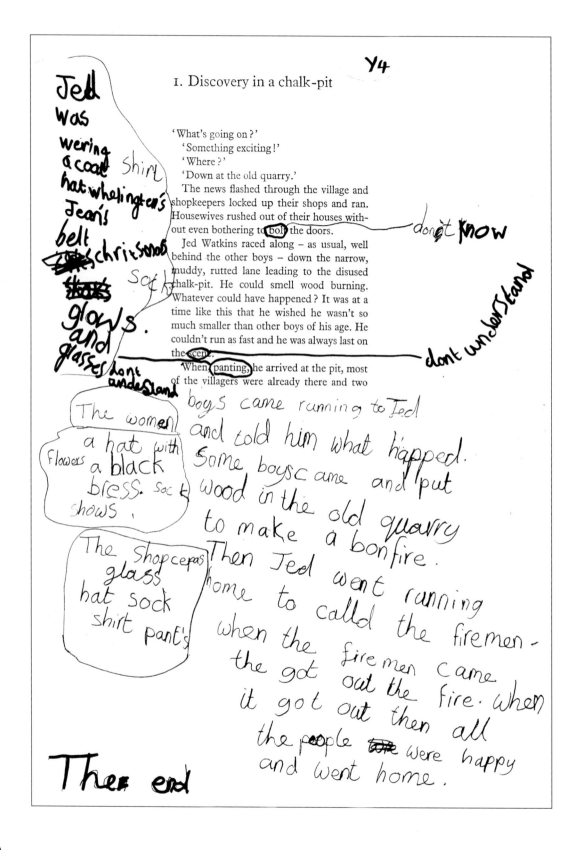

Y4

1. Discovery in a chalk-pit

'What's going on?'
'Something exciting!'
'Where?'
'Down at the old quarry.'
The news flashed through the village and shopkeepers locked up their shops and ran. Housewives rushed out of their houses without even bothering to bolt the doors.

Jed Watkins raced along – as usual, well behind the other boys – down the narrow, muddy, rutted lane leading to the disused chalk-pit. He could smell wood burning. Whatever could have happened? It was at a time like this that he wished he wasn't so much smaller than other boys of his age. He couldn't run as fast and he was always last on the scene.

When, panting, he arrived at the pit, most of the villagers were already there and two

Jed was wering a coat shirt hat wheling ter's Jeans belt chrisms Soc gloves and glasses dont anderstand

dont know
dont understand

The women a hat with Flowers a black bress. Soc shows.

The Shopcepas glass hat sock shirt pant's

boys came running to Jed and told him what happed. Some boys came and put wood in the old quarry to make a bonfire. Then Jed went running home to calld the firemen. when the firemen came the got out the fire. When it got out then all the people were were happy and went home.

Thee end

they do not understand and then describe how they 'picture' the setting and the characters.

It is fascinating to see which words have been circled as not being understood and wonder why. Do they know that 'Watkins' is Jed's surname or perhaps an adverb describing how he raced ('quickly raced'). Have they ever heard of a chalk pit or a rutted lane or a quarry? Again we see how reading requires vocabulary but also how it can provide vocabulary through the discussion of pieces of writing. The children's descriptions of the place and people show their responses going way beyond what is offered in the text. This really is gap filling! Examples from a number of pairs will then be used as the basis of discussing what the author does tell us and where the different responses came from.

In the second example Mudassar and Asad have continued the story (from half way through a sentence!). Their writing shows comprehension of the passage they have read and could lead to useful discussions in which they compared what they had produced with efforts from other pairs.

There are many other books and guides with detailed ideas for exploring these areas with children (see Chapter 18) and wonderful work can result from using drama, art, music and dance. It is not the intention of this book to provide lists of ideas. What we have tried to do is explore the underlying rationale for whatever work is organised:

That reading is about active readers interacting with stories both in terms of themselves and the text.

That the more experience children gain of a particular type of text the more literary competence they build which helps them read the next example of that type of text.

Reading can lead to writing

Throughout this book the connections between speaking, listening, reading and writing are emphasised as we manage what the National Curriculum refers to as 'an integrated programme' of English. A Blocked Unit of work based around a set of short stories will not only give children a varied experience of narrative but can also form the basis of different types of writing. Through such writing children can:

- engage with the stories so as to gain a deeper appreciation of what they are about and how they work;
- learn about the features of different types of written text. This modelling of writing on reading is rightly stressed in the National Literacy Strategy.

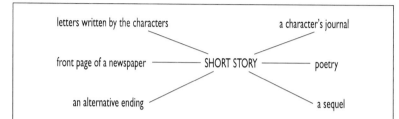

As an example we could take Joan Aiken's 'A Necklace of Raindrops' (say with a Y3 class):
- the last few pages can be left unread so that the children can write their own ending and compare them to the original;
- sequels such as 'return of the North Wind' or 'Meg's Revenge' can be written; (Here we are providing children with tremendous support for their own stories — far easier than constantly being faced with a blank page. Already provided are characters, settings, even a style for those capable of attempting to imitate it.)
- imagine Laura had kept a journal during the action of the story . . . ;
- how would a newspaper have reported the story?
- imagine that Laura and the princess wrote to each other after the end of the story . . . ;
- what would a necklace of raindrops have looked like/felt like . . . poems, perhaps haikus or cinquaines.

Three problems you may need to address

Comprehension
Course books using extracts
The Y6 SAT

As a coordinator you may well find one or more of three problems in your school which will get in the way of the high quality teaching you are seeking to establish.

1 **Comprehension**
It may be that regular doses of 'comprehension' are administered in the mistaken belief that these exercises actually help to develop reading skills. It is to be hoped that 'independent' work in the literacy hour is not dominated by reams of 'comprehension' exercises. In fact, comprehension exercises have a place in the assessment of reading but it does not follow that weekly assessment will bring about

improvement. We must not confuse assessment techniques with teaching strategies. Reading lessons should involve **teaching**; children exploring and discussing texts, and teachers moving the work on at pace and introducing new ideas and vocabulary as and when necessary. The danger is that your colleagues will view the work described above as an extra — something to do in addition to other work, rather than something which replaces it. Then it quickly becomes marginalised rather than an established part of English teaching. Before too long it has all but disappeared. However, response work is actually 'comprehension', much more so than the weekly exercises masquerading under the title in some schools. Through it children investigate their own reading and from there the ways in which different texts work. If this is an issue in your school it is worth considering whether you refer to such work as 'comprehension' rather than 'response' when planning it with colleagues!

2 **Course books using extracts**

Allied to the above problem is that of course books which present a couple of pages from a novel as the passage for comprehension work. In real life we never read the middle two pages of a novel before having read the previous pages! The exercise is so artificial that children soon learn to treat it as such rather than as a real reading exercise (we can all remember doing this when we were at school — being told to read the whole passage first, but realising that this just wasted time as the answer to the first question was bound to be near the beginning and the answer to the second question . . . !). In fact this problem is not difficult to address given that it is now fear of the Y6 SAT which drives such work. In terms of literature, the SAT uses whole texts — a whole short story and a whole poem. Children are far more likely to gain good SAT results if they work in class on whole short stories rather than extracts. If we want to work on aspects of novels then the obvious part to focus on is the opening — the first couple of paragraphs, as suggested above.

3 **The Y6 SAT**

There is a real danger that fear of the Y6 SAT will backwash on to the whole of the Key Stage 2 English curriculum. The argument seems to be that because there is a reading test (really a comprehension test) then children must be subjected to constant comprehension exercises during the preceding three and a half years. In fact such an approach will not produce the desired results. What are far more likely to work are the ideas discussed above. A six week Blocked Unit of work in each year at Key Stage 2, based each time around the reading and exploring of half a dozen short stories will mean that by the time the children reach the Y6 SAT they will have examined 24 short stories. Similar Blocked Units for poetry, each one exploring say, a dozen poems, will mean children experiencing 48 poems. The short story and poem in the SAT will then be just further examples. Children will know *how* to approach them, *how* to read them, *how* to find their way around them. They will have developed the **literary competence** necessary to read these texts. When children have difficulty with answering the questions, the reasons may lie somewhat deeper than we think. They may just not have had the necessary reading experience. While we would want such work established for reasons far beyond crude notions of SAT results and league tables (because it will develop children as readers in a much wider sense), these reasons can be used with some colleagues to influence their practice. So much of English teaching is concerned with constantly revisiting areas and using the vocabulary of the subject — a sort of drip feed approach. Once teachers begin to work like this they understand what English teaching is in fact all about.

This discussion of the potential of short stories has focused on four key areas. These areas are equally important for approaching novels in the KS2 classroom and should form the basis of any work with them:

1   Teachers should read aloud thus modelling the reading for children — 'this is how such a piece of writing should be read'.
2   Literary texts should be discussed — the basis of such discussion is the shared enthusiasm of both teacher and children.
3   Literary texts can be investigated — both in terms of the reader's response and the ways in which the texts work.
4   Reading can lead to writing.

As coordinator it is important to establish how these will impact on the practice in your school.

Poetry

As coordinator, you may find yourself faced with a challenging situation in terms of establishing poetry as a regular and valued aspect of the curriculum. In our experience there can be three problems which may have to be addressed:

1 In some classrooms poetry is marginalised in the sense that it rarely appears in its own right. In these classrooms it will often be tagged on to the current topic, so that the topic is central and the poetry only valued in so far as it contributes to it. If we are studying explorers and navigators then we can have some 'sea poems'.

2 In many classrooms children are fed a diet of 'light verse', based around the amusing poetry of Michael Rosen, Alan Ahlberg, Roald Dahl, Spike Milligan and others. Indeed some children must leave for secondary school convinced that poetry is always funny! We have nothing against any of these writers, who should always be part of the 'balanced reading diet' referred to elsewhere, but there is much, much more to poetry.

3 Poetry can make an appearance as no more than another 'comprehension exercise'. A written text followed by a list of questions. As emphasised above this is not a teaching technique, more an assessment exercise, and in the case of poetry can give children the idea that poems are no more than difficult puzzles which require the answering of difficult questions if their mysteries are to be unravelled. This could be a major issue in the use of poems in literacy hours.

In many schools these problems have long been left far behind but if any of them strikes a chord in terms of your situation the underlying reason may well be that the teachers themselves are unsure about how to approach poetry with children so that **the poetic experience is valued for its own sake**. In order to discover what is happening in the classrooms in your school, **an audit** of practice will be necessary. This can lead to a development plan for poetry in the school based on the key idea that:

We read poems more than once. When we have finished a novel we rarely turn immediately to the first page and start again! Yet this is exactly what we often do with a poem. It is as if the first reading has simply been an orientation exercise. There may well have been a very powerful response as a result of this first encounter, involving connections with one's own life, a feeling for what the poet is trying to communicate, particular words/phrases/lines which stand out, an awareness of how the poem has been constructed. Depending on the poem one or more of these will dominate but they all hit the reader at once. Now we feel the need for a second or third or even fourth reading. Our original response may remain or even deepen (we may have re-read the poem simply to confirm it) but through these repeated readings we begin to separate out all those things which were merged in the first reading. The poem begins to reveal itself.

If the above paragraph represents normal reading behaviour when we are faced with the first reading of a poem surely it ought to be the basis of how we 'teach' poetry in the classroom. Perhaps one of the major reasons 'challenging' poems are so often shied away from is because teachers recognise how difficult they are for children. But this 'difficulty' is so often due to 'comprehension questions' (either verbal or written) being posed after only one reading. Indeed the child can be struggling with question one only a few seconds after having finished the poem! Poems then become 'difficult', puzzles to be solved rather than powerful reading experiences. Safer to stick with the funny ones.

If you are trying to establish poetry in its own right in your school there are two effective approaches which are worth considering. Both address the issue of re-reading and 'comprehension' and result in children gaining an understanding of the power of poems and the enjoyment which can be gained from discussing them.

A poem a day

On Monday morning the day begins with a poem read aloud by the teacher. At the end of the reading there is a thirty second pause. Silence. No chat. No questions. Then the 'day' begins.

Tuesday begins with the same poem. Wednesday with a different one. Over the course of a fortnight, two or three poems will each be read three or four times. By the final readings children will often be observed silently 'joining in' with parts they remember. The poems begin to sort themselves out in their minds.

Now small groups can be formed to discuss the poems. Copies of each are made available. Firstly the group reads each poem — perhaps taking it in turns and helping each other through, perhaps one child volunteering to read, perhaps a pair of children reading together. The repeat readings from the teacher have provided a 'map' of the texts and a model for how they ought to be read; the pace, rhythm, intonation.

Discussion of the poems (just as with stories) needs to focus on both the reader and the text.

Reader
- How did the poems make us feel? What effect did they have on us?
- What did the poems make us think about?
- Did the poems produce any 'pictures in the mind'?

Which particular words/phrases/lines/verses are important in considering our responses? Is there any indication of the poet who wrote it? Do we know how she or he feels or why they wrote it?

Text
- Which words/phrases/lines/verses have you particularly remembered?
- Are there any words/phrases/lines/verses which you do not understand? Can any of the group help?
- Are there any patterns in the poems?
  Patterns on the page e.g. the poem divided into verses:
  - rhymes and rhythms;
  - alliteration or assonance;
  - repeated refrains.

If each of the poems is copied onto A3 paper and the group provided with coloured pens or text highlighters, the discussions can be recorded and parts of the poems underlined or circled or coloured. Groups can pass their sheets around and see whether other groups have responded in exactly the same way. Reviewing with the whole class, the teacher can point out further aspects of the poems which the children may have missed. This sort of approach will work extremely well in the Literacy Hour.

There is no need to worry about whether each poem has been totally 'taught'. This is not the aim of the work. The results will only become apparent as children move up through KS2 engaging with poetry regularly on this basis. A dozen poems can be examined each term. Between thirty and forty in a year. Over one hundred by Y6! Now, presented with a poem, children approach it on the basis of experience. They 'know' about poetry — how it ought to be read, its characteristics, its power. Like adults who have read poetry, they can switch to 'poem mode' when presented with a poem.

Poetry and voice — the sound of language

A second way in which repeated reading of a poem can allow children to 'work it out' before they discuss it is by having them 'perform' a poem with their voices. Once they have taken part in this exercise they are able to work in small groups on further poems, but for the teacher who is unsure about poetry (or the class with not much experience of 'serious', challenging poetry) the whole class 'lesson' is the best way to begin. The key again is the quality of the teacher's reading, modelling for children the way the poem should be read.

Children are given their own copies of the poem and then follow the text as the teacher reads it aloud. After a short pause (but no discussion) the poem is read aloud again. The class is now presented with the challenge — that it will be able to 'perform' the poem *without scripts* by the end of the session. Children love challenges!

Someone volunteers or is chosen to read the title and author. Then with a mixture of single voices, pairs, threes, larger groupings of voices the performance of the poem is orchestrated by the teacher. Everyone can join in. Confident children with the capability of doing so can read parts alone. Less confident children or struggling readers can join groupings. As the poem builds, a number of things must be borne in mind if the exercise is to have full impact:

■ keep going back to the beginning of the poem as each new part is added. This way the children will have heard and participated in it many times by the end;

■ don't be afraid to 'coach' voices. Reading poetry is about the pauses as much as the words between them. Some words are 'elastic' in the way we speak them, stretching their sound for maximum effect. Pace and volume vary;

■ Position children around the room so that the voices constantly switch from place to place creating dramatic effects.

More often than not the challenge is successfully met. Occasionally more time is required. Always the poem is returned to the next day or later in the week to be performed again, perhaps for the benefit of other children or parents. The poem becomes 'known' by the children and can then be discussed in the ways described above. But it is a very different text now to the poem they heard on its first reading. Discussing it now is a different exercise from having to do so after just that one reading.

There are excellent books of ideas for poetry on the market (see Chapter 18) with lovely ideas for using art, music, dance, movement . . . We have focused on the above two because they are concerned with the poetry itself and because they illustrate important ideas which all KS2 teachers need to appreciate about the demands of poetry and the need for children to experience it regularly in its different forms if they are to develop the literary competence necessary to read it and appreciate it for them selves.

Classic poetry — Wordsworth in Key Stage 2

The National Curriculum states that children should read some classic texts before they leave the primary school. Our experience suggests that this is an even greater challenge than those described above in that it introduces an extra dimension — teacher knowledge. A poem by a living poet can be approached as we have suggested, simply as a text. We may seek out a profile of the poet from such journals as 'Books For Keeps' but these tend to contain personal information which, while interesting, may not influence the way we set about the poem. However with, say, Wordsworth, there is something more. Who was he? When did he live? Why exactly is he an important poet? Teacher knowledge at KS2 in other curriculum subjects has been recognised as a major issue. How can we be 'experts' on everything from the refraction of light to the ancient Egyptians? And now there is knowledge of the history of English Literature to be added.

The approach outlined below is definitely based on teacher knowledge as will be seen, but more than that is an imaginative approach to poetry which has application beyond the particular poem being discussed. We are grateful to Nancy Martin, Education Officer at the Wordsworth Trust for permission to print her materials.

The poem we have chosen is the most famous written by Wordsworth — in fact untitled, but known as 'Daffodils'. The first piece of teacher knowledge is that the actual seeing of the 'host of golden daffodils' took place some two years before Wordsworth wrote about it!

'Daffodils' by William Wordsworth

Here is Dorothy's journal entry:

When we were in the woods beyond Gowbarrow park we saw a few daffodils close to the water side, we fancied that the lake had floated the seeds ashore & that the little colony had so sprung up — But as we went along there were more & yet more & at last under the boughs of the trees, we saw that there was a long belt of them along the shore, about the breadth of a country turnpike road. I never saw daffodils so beautiful they grew among the mossy stones about & about them, some rested their heads upon these stones as on a pillow for weariness & the rest tossed & reeled & danced & seemed as if they verily laughed with the wind that blew upon them over the Lake, they looked so gay ever glancing ever changing. This wind blew directly over the Lake to them. There was here & there a little knot & a few stragglers a few yards higher up but they were so few as not to disturb the simplicity & unity & life of that one busy highway...

Dorothy Wordsworth, *Journal*, 15th April 1802

Now here is Wordsworth's poem:

'I wandered lonely as a Cloud'

I wandered lonely as a Cloud
That floats on high o'er Vales and Hills,
When all at once I saw a crowd,
A host of golden Daffodils;
Beside the Lake, beneath the trees,
Fluttering and dancing in the breeze.

Continuous as the stars that shine
And twinkle on the milky way,
They stretched in never-ending line
Along the margin of a bay:
Ten thousand saw I at a glance,
Tossing their heads in sprightly dance.

The waves beside them danced, but they
Out-did the sparkling waves in glee: —
A Poet could not but be gay
In such a jocund company:
I gazed — and gazed — but little thought
What wealth the shew to me had brought:

For oft when on my I couch I lie
In vacant or in pensive mood,
They flash upon that inward eye
Which is the bliss of solitude,
And then my heart with pleasure fills,
And dances with the Daffodils.

Published in *Collected Poems*, 1815

With nothing further to go on, the potential for imaginative classwork is clearly present comparing a prose account with a poem about the same event. In what ways are they similar or different?

Here are Nancy Martin's notes for teachers:

The Poems

'Daffodils'

Points to consider

Wordsworth wrote his poem two years after he actually saw the daffodils and clearly it is based on Dorothy's account, which was written at the time. It was not unusual for Wordsworth to get ideas from his sister's journal, in fact she began it because she hoped to 'give Wm pleasure by it'. However, as well as recording potential subject-matter for William's poems, Dorothy obviously derived great personal satisfaction from her descriptions: imaginative and evocative passages such as this, indicate her own pleasure and fascination with the process of writing.

Dorothy's description

Dorothy's journal account captures a moment in time and helps us to picture what she saw. The constant repetition of the word 'and' (or &, as she always shortens it) gives the description an immediate, almost breathless feel, which evokes the storminess of the day (they had difficulty in walking against the wind, which 'was furious & . . . seized our breath'). The impression of the strong wind is also conveyed by the many movements of the daffodils which toss, reel, dance, laugh etc.

Dorothy uses *personification* — she gives the flowers human characteristics. Flowers cannot laugh or dance, but describing them like this helps us to imagine what they might have looked like.

Wordsworth's poem

Wordsworth wrote the first version of his poem in 1804, two years after they saw the daffodils. His aim is not to give an accurate description of what he saw, but to work out how he can remember the flowers after such a long time. His poem is about memory and imagination.

Although at first sight, the words and phrases he uses seem very close to Dorothy's, they are in fact, very different. In his imagination the daffodils increase vastly in number (they are continuous and never-ending) and, while Dorothy's flowers are doing all sorts of different things in the gale-force wind, Wordsworth's appear more sedate and organised and are in a much more gentle breeze — none of his flowers rest or straggle! The most obvious alteration that Wordsworth makes, is to imagine he was alone and not with Dorothy.

The second and third sentences take us to the heart of Wordsworth's aim as a poet, but accessible to primary children.

Now, though, there is further information:

'Daffodils' — Did You Know . . . ?

- Wordsworth's 'Daffodils' is one of the most famous and widely read poems in the English language.
- Wordsworth never gave his poem a title, but it is now generally known as 'Daffodils'.
- Daffodils were probably not Wordsworth's favourite flower. If he had a favourite, it might have been the celandine, (or common pilewort). He wrote no less than three poems about these tiny, wild flowers which bloom in the early spring. This is the first verse of *To the small Celandine*:

> Pansies, lilies, kingcups, daisies,
> Let them live upon their praises;
> Long as there's a sun that sets,
> Primroses will have their glory;
> Long as there are violets,
> They will have a place in story:
> There's a flower that shall be mine,
> 'Tis the little Celandine.

- As with many of his poems, Wordsworth had second thoughts about 'Daffodils'. His first version, with three verses, was written in 1804, but he published another version in 1815, with the addition of a new verse ('Continuous as the stars . . . '). He also made some changes to verse one:

First version	Second version
I wandered lonely as a Cloud	I wandered lonely as a Cloud
That floats on high o'er Vales and Hills,	That floats on high o'er Vales and Hills,
When all at once I saw a crowd	When all at once I saw a crowd,
A host of dancing Daffodils;	A host of golden Daffodils;
Along the Lake, beneath the trees,	Beside the Lake, beneath the trees,
Ten thousand dancing in the breeze.	Fluttering and dancing in the breeze.

- When he was an old man, Wordsworth recalled writing 'Daffodils' and admitted that 'The two best lines in it are by Mary' (his wife). Most people think the two best lines are in the last verse, which describe how, in quiet moments, he can suddenly remember the daffodils and re-live the original pleasure he had when he first saw them:

> They flash upon that inward eye
> Which is the bliss of solitude . . .

So we can move from the 'simple' (Wordsworth's favourite flower) to the fascinating (his wife wrote the two best lines . . . and his sister wrote the original prose account) and the original version was revised (redrafted!) eleven years later.

This approach to the work of a classic author has so much more to offer than simply presenting a poem to children simply because it is a classic. The danger is that the poem can become a dead thing which we feel children should simply 'know about' rather than a living piece of writing which evolved in different ways.

Chapter 6   Speaking and listening

Background

As the TTA expectations for subject leaders emphasise, to be an effective coordinator it is essential that you have a strong grasp of the subject. A clear understanding of the central issues will help with the task of supporting others and developing the curriculum in school. This applies to all subjects but, in the case of English, the impact of subject knowledge is significant since English influences all the other subjects.

Speaking and listening are central to progress in English. Talk precedes reading and writing and influences their development. By exploring the issues relating to speaking and listening and recognising the challenge in teaching pupils, the role of the coordinator becomes apparent.

Speaking and listening are dealt with in some depth for another, important, reason. Their impact in the classroom and upon children goes further than English and upon other subjects. Speaking and listening have enormous influence upon children's confidence, personal growth and the development of social skills. Developing these personal qualities in children is often at the very heart of a school's aims. Schools state their intention to enable children to become confident, independent, responsible and tolerant; these qualities are very much caught. They depend on children being put into situations where they can experience and exercise their developing qualities and, in so many cases, that means becoming more effective users of speaking and listening.

The role of the subject leader in English at Key Stage 2, therefore, demands an awareness of the issues related to speaking and listening.

KS2 Speaking and listening

Meeting the demands of the National Curriculum in terms of the speaking and listening Programmes of Study at Key Stage 2 is both easy and difficult at the same time. On the surface it should be easy in contemporary schools to give children every opportunity to develop in the area of speaking and listening. In practice it is extremely difficult to move forward from offering opportunities into actually teaching the children what they need to know and be able to do about speaking and listening.

Speaking and listening are natural

Of all the other areas in all the other subjects speaking and listening is surely the most natural thing that children bring to school. Almost all children in mainstream primary school can talk and listen to varying degrees. They do it outside school in the home, in the community, for entertainment, for leisure, and hence when they come to school one of the challenges facing the teacher is to help children realise that they need to take turns to listen as well as speak and sometimes to be quiet so that the teacher can talk. The children who succeed in speaking and listening are those who know how to manage their own contribution, the ones who know the difference between speaking and listening and those who know when to speak and when to listen.

Speaking and listening have conventions

Much of the challenge of helping children to come to terms with the conventions of speaking in a class of 30 plus children has already been met by the time children get to Key Stage 2, but the children who have not grasped the key understandings about how to control their own talking within the classroom by the time they get to the age of 7 are often the children who have most difficulty in coming to terms with the social world in which they spend so much of their school day.

If speaking and listening are so natural, the argument might follow that children should be encouraged to meet the expectations of the National Curriculum in a natural way within the classroom. If the classroom is flexible, easy going, a real working environment where children need to take responsibility for themselves, their work and their property, then it would be natural that they would be engaged in interactions with other people and therefore developing speaking and listening skills.

The challenge for the teacher though is not just to provide the environment where speaking and listening can take place but to move the quality of speaking and listening on so that the pupils make progress. Is it acceptable for children, even in the normal social world of the classroom, to be managing their own resources with phrases such as 'here give me that' or 'I want that, you can't have it' or 's'mine, you're not having it' or 'can I have the thingy what er you use for the er what's it to the er doings'? Or should it be that we expect children to express themselves more clearly and manage their interactions more skilfully so that as they move into secondary school and the adult world beyond, they are able to feel more secure and confident and perhaps gain more respect from others?

Speaking and listening opportunities

Whereas other subjects need to seek a context, for purpose, process and audience and need to find places and events in which to make the subject 'real', speaking and listening should have no problem. The whole school curriculum, indeed the whole school world, provides opportunities for pupils to engage in and develop and make progress in their abilities in speaking and listening. The environments in which they spend their days, whether the classroom, the hall, the corridor, the dining room, assembly or the play ground, are all places where children will speak and listen. The challenge for the teaching staff is to construct experiences within the school day which positively affect children as they use the speaking and listening, which are so natural, to more greatly influence the school world in which they live.

The Literacy Framework emphasisis the importance of speaking and listening within the context of the Literacy Hour. The strategies to be used include

■ discussing and arguing: e.g. to put points of view, argue a case, justify a prefernce;

■ listening to and responding: e.g. to stimulate and extend pupils' contributions, to discuss/evaluate the presentations.

Speaking and listening — range in the National Curriculum

When we read words in the National Curriculum such as *range*, in terms of speaking and listening, it can mean virtually anything. The National Curriculum document provides six bullet points of examples that are offered as a range of purposes and contain 18 examples of opportunities that could be offered. The National Curriculum says pupils should be given opportunities to communicate to different audiences and reflect on how speakers adapt their vocabulary, tone, pace and style. Such a sentence contains so many challenges for the teacher! For instance, if we think of some of the more notable pop stars and sporting heroes that regularly appear on the television there would seem to be relatively little effort made by some of them to adapt anything and yet they still receive adulation, attention and considerable sums of money. Contrast this with some members of the community who speak with clear diction, use beautiful vocabulary, pace their talk in an interesting way but find themselves mocked for being old-fashioned, fuddy duddy and out of date and we see the dilemma facing the teacher in the Key Stage 2 classroom at the present time.

Models for speaking and listening

When teachers are asked to be 'models' for their children, the model sometimes displayed goes counter to the very background of the children and to those presented by the media as being worthwhile. Perhaps this area is dealt with in the Programme of Study, when we are asked to give opportunities to children to identify and comment on key features of what they see and hear in a variety of media. Perhaps as well as looking at advertisements or political persuasion we are expected to be teaching children to be able to infer which people are inherently good, and which are inherently poor as models for the society we are supposedly trying to encourage.

Drama

It is within the area of speaking and listening that drama emerges as one of the subjects that cannot seem to find a home. Within this area, children are to be offered opportunities to participate and respond in a variety of forms so that they are able to evaluate contributions. This means that we can exploit the enjoyment most children get from play and using fantasy and simulations to set contexts in which they can explore different forms and purposes for speaking and listening. By working in role, in a reconstruction of a situation from a time in a Victorian workhouse, children can gain more empathy with the people of that era. By being placed in the situation of the famous figures of history and asked to reconstruct famous events children can visualise some of the stories they read and some of the alternative outcomes that were avoided for whatever reason. The challenge for the teacher is to make such drama 'real' rather than just 'play', so that there is impact upon learning. Many children in Key Stage 2 will at some point find themselves in a mock Victorian classroom with a fierce teacher, punishments, lots of chanting, and dunce's caps. Most children enjoy these events and some say they wish school could always be like this! The role play has not given them the background conditions of the children they represent. They are not poor, undernourished, living in homes with no sanitation, urchin-like characters like some of the Victorians. Most of their parents want them at school whereas many Victorians wanted their children out earning and not wasting time at school. The children in role can get a superficial image of the scene through role play and, unless really exploited, such activities can only give an illustration or a flavour. Good teaching will draw out the underlying issues, expose the language appropriate to the situation, and move the children's understanding on, both in speaking and listening and in the subject being studied.

The good teaching includes effective review. In all curriculum areas, children are more likely to learn if we help them to review what they have been learning. In drama, the opportunity to reflect with others on the drama, to respond, to criticise and to suggest alternatives will make a learning experience matter. Applause is a form of appreciation and appropriate sometimes, but children need to learn the habit of reviewing and trying to develop so that they appreciate the point of the medium.

Teaching speaking and listening

For the teacher at Key Stage 2 the challenge in developing good speaking and listening opportunities lies in not simply providing the 'natural' and hoping that children will grow and develop as speakers and listeners, but providing the situations which will enable children to make progress through quality teaching. As with reading and writing it is not sufficient to provide the experience and leave the children to get on with it. What is necessary is for the teacher to structure, control and intervene in children's learning at appropriate points, just as with reading and writing, so that learning can be seized upon and exploited. Speaking and listening demand

■ as much planning and as much attention to detail as reading and writing;

■ that delicate balance between teacher direction and allowing the children to work independently that is essential in the early stages of writing and reading;

■ the close control and attention to detail that is necessary when helping children to structure their writing or make sense of their reading;

■ exactly the same kind of precision that is necessary when teachers mark or respond to children's writing or reading;

■ the careful assessment and interpretation that allows the child to move ahead and make sense of what they are doing, even though they are making some errors.

With good teaching, the context and the search for meaning lead the child to want to make the experience matter and try to improve.

This is why when it comes to key skills within the Programme of Study for Key Stage 2, the key phrases all contain the word 'taught'. Speaking and listening will just happen but children will not necessarily make progress unless some teaching occurs; so children need to be taught to organise what they want to say. They need to be taught

- to evaluate their own talk;
- to listen carefully and to identify the gist of an account and;
- to listen to others and be able to question meaning, extend and follow-up ideas.

It is this teaching which is the challenge for teachers within the classroom in terms of structure, context, purpose, process and audience.

As speaking and listening is interpreted through the Standard English and Language Study element, the National Curriculum appears to be somewhat vague. The teacher is expected to help children appreciate Standard English through providing activities that demand a range of grammatical constructions and vocabulary. The problem is that teachers can find the setting but, without teaching the aspects mentioned previously, children will not be able to respond in Standard English. Equally, there are many situations when a response which is natural and a million miles away from Standard English would be absolutely appropriate. However, the sense of it and the implications borne within a couple of paragraphs are enormously difficult to develop, so we get vague blandness where children are going to extend their vocabulary by discussing more imaginative and adventurous choices of words. One would only have to sit with some groups of 11-year-olds and listen to their conversations when they presume no adult is around to hear that they are not needing more imaginative and adventurous choices of words! Indeed some would argue that they would be better with a restricted choice of words.

Developing good practice in speaking and listening

The teacher's responsibility is to plan for effective speaking and listening in the classroom; the challenge is how to do it.

The notion of providing opportunities is a good starting point and we can think about some of the examples for the requirements of the Programmes of Study. If we are expected to give pupils opportunities to express their ideas to a range of audiences there are lots of ways we can do it. For example, we can see experiences as gradually moving 'out' from the child:

- children can talk to small groups about the work they have been doing, such as building a model, designing an experiment, or writing a story;

- children can participate in 'circle time', where the children are encouraged to talk about their feelings, problems and difficulties as well as their successes and achievements, as a way of encouraging the growth of the relationships as part of a personal health and social education programme;

- children can provide short talks for their class on their interests, hobbies or work they have been doing, using the rest of the class as the audience;

- children can welcome adult visitors to the school and show them around explaining their perceptions of how the school works;

- children can talk or read aloud during assembly.

All of these are examples of ways in which schools extend to pupils opportunities for talking. However, extending the opportunity does not lead to progress unless the teacher's intervention is sensitive, controlled and timely. This demands great skill on the part of the teacher and is sometimes taken for granted when perhaps it should not be. How many adults can take part fully in a group discussion with equal opportunity for all to speak when the number in the group goes above 10?

Most schools work hard to give children speaking and listening opportunities. Yet, they so often seem to start from the big picture, the furthest point from the child. Some of the opportunities mentioned are provided in most schools, but one of the key questions is related to who takes the opportunity. In many schools we only have to sit with a small group of children to see who would usually be chosen to take significant roles in leading assemblies. Everyone knows which

To take another example, such as helping children to understand the need to adapt their speech to different situations. It might be possible for the children to consider practising small role play situations where they experience a problem. For instance they may have lost a piece of equipment and need to ask various people whether it has been found. Alternatively, they could have found a piece of equipment belonging to somebody else and could consider the ways in which language can be used to try to ascertain the owner. The simulation could be taken forward into the wider world to consider how we might take back a faulty product such as a camera to a shop and explain the problems with the purchase. Again children could work through the sorts of conversations that might be necessary to ask directions, buy tickets or deal with a problem at the cycle repairers. All of these examples present images of our approaches to learning a modern foreign language which involve finding the context and rehearsing the situation that may occur. As many of us know, the simulation is wonderful until you get into the real situation. Asking the question is simple, understanding the answer is sometimes where we get lost! Again the use of other adults, classroom assistants, students, work experience pupils from the secondary school or parents provides a real sounding board for children to experience proper conversations, even in the simulation, rather than the stilted 'let's pretend' world that often exists in our schools.

ones have the charisma, self confidence and the aplomb to stand up in front of the rest of their school and talk easily. One of the problems is that the more these particular children do it, the better they become, and the less the others do it, the less progress they make; yet we need these good ones to carry the assemblies. Of course we could argue it is differentiation in its full form. The better children are taking responsibility, the less secure are playing the bit parts. The danger is that, just as in reading, the slow reader gets slower, so in speaking aloud to an audience, the struggler continues to struggle.

Yet isn't it a demanding situation to be placed in? So many children can stand up in front of two, three, four hundred others and speak coherently with good intonation and expression about something of interest and yet many adults would find such situations daunting.

Whilst most people can see the difficulties of using assembly as a vehicle for developing speaking and listening, it is easy to overlook the similar impact of being asked to show a visitor around the school. Some people are at ease in talking to two or three hundred others, while others are at ease at the level of a one to one conversation. Sometimes the opportunity to show a visitor around is threatening for the children involved unless the adult is experienced in handling such situations.

These examples show the difficulty of simply creating opportunities without moving on from there and doing the teaching that lies behind them. No-one would expect children to stand up in front of assembly without some preparation and practise time before hand, so maybe it's important that we provide preparation and practise time for all the other situations that are suggested above. Perhaps the teacher should provide a structure that could be used by children when they show a visitor around the school. So if we are working with the children maybe as a class, maybe in groups

They could:
- highlight the important features that need to be pointed out;
- think of an appropriate route around the school;
- think of some sensible things to ask a visitor;
- think of conversation starters;

- consider what to do if time is short;
- consider how to cope if there are problems encountered during the walk about.

Given such planning children would develop confidence and when called upon to take part in such an exercise may be able to achieve more than simply walking around like a blind person's guide dog with little to say except 'This is the way we are going'. Practising on a parent or known adult might inspire confidence, with child and adult reviewing the exercise afterwards. Just as in reading or writing, the teacher has to think how to help the children use these natural opportunities to extend their learning, so it is with speaking and listening.

What becomes apparent is that it is possible to provide lessons in speaking and listening in order to help children develop, as well as provide the environment in which they can experience speaking and listening opportunities. The lessons are the structured steps that will help the children to gain from the experiences offered. The steps have to be carefully considered, for sometimes they have to come in the right order.

Just as children need support in making progress within their speech, so they need help within the area of listening. Again listening opportunities are fine but unless children are given the opportunity to learn how to listen they simply do lots more listening. Good listeners get better at listening, poor listeners get worse at listening and the gulf between them widens just as with good readers and poor readers. In fact, if listening is a central aspect of so many classrooms, then the more we can help children to learn to listen the better the outcome in all the curriculum areas might be. Again as well as intervening, being sensitive, using situations as they arise, helping children to listen carefully within a context, it is important that the teacher makes explicit the fact that we are trying to help the children to learn to listen more effectively.

Within Key Stage 2 it is reasonable to set the children challenges to see:
- whether they can follow instructions;
- whether they can hear how many sentences exist in a short passage;

Suggestion

Looking at the aspect of language study with reference to speaking and listening is possible in all sorts of settings within the school. For example, a link with data handling might occur if children were to investigate the different forms of language used in different parts of the school. Starting points might be the playground, the dining room, the library, headteacher's office, secretary's room, classroom, the staff room even if we could allow eavesdroppers! If children were encouraged to make a display, perhaps including photographs or some commentaries, speeches in bubbles, they could bring alive the study of language. This could then be explored through the use of graphs and charts to show the incidents of the use of certain phrases, colloquialisms, jokes, questions, instructions and so on. If we want children to see that different language is appropriate in different situations opportunity to study it in its spoken form is vital. This is where effective planning pulls things together. This investigation would be a unit of work within the speaking and listening programme 'linked' with data handling.

- whether they can predict the rhyme at the end of a series of rhyming couplets;
- whether they can suggest the end to a limerick;
- whether they can remember a series of details from a short passage read to them;
- whether they can select the three most important points from a short talk or a video extract on television.

All of these possibilities and others present the children with the opportunity to develop their listening skills and improve their concentration during 'taught times' so that when they have to apply the skill of listening within other contexts they gradually become more able to do so.

Many of the good examples of the teaching of speaking and listening in the classroom would be carried out under the notion of 'on-going' units of work within planning. They are the aspects that need to be addressed over and over again through Key Stage 1 and onwards. Most teachers would argue that they encourage speaking and listening opportunities all the way through. Most teachers would argue that one of the big problems is to help children to listen more and stop them talking so much! The challenge though is not merely to provide the opportunities but to teach and to plan regular on-going units of work that drip, drip, drip on the children so that their progress in the curriculum develops.

Opportunities in other areas of the curriculum

The further challenge is to use speaking and learning skills within other curriculum areas and give children the chance to practise and put into context the skill they are learning. So within science children might get opportunities to plan, predict and investigate together. In English they might make use of sharing ideas in stories or for example having insights and opinions about a poem. Within history we might be exploring, developing, explaining ideas of the development of motor transport through the arrangement of pictures in a timeline sequence. In such examples we need to make speaking and listening the explicit focus at points within the teaching so that children are thinking about it. By creating natural links it is possible for children not to realise how they are using speaking and listening or to recognise how they are developing. We need to regularly ask children to review the ways they have been using language, the techniques, the subtleties, the turning points and the confusions. In doing so we give the children extended practise in speaking and listening but also fulfil that significant part of the subject leader's job which is to see the possibility of linking English to the wider benefit and development of the child. As children work together through effective speaking and listening they gain opportunities to negotiate, experience give and take, justify, stand by their own view point, and fight their corner. All of these are essential skills that children will need as they grow into adulthood. To be a member of a society means to take part and English, especially in speaking and listening, is the key to social development and skills for so many children. Well-structured lessons which make best use of speaking and listening will open doors to so many children. In doing this we will be working on speaking and listening in the areas closest to the children. The problem for the coordinator is that teachers are more reluctant to teach speaking and listening as a natural part of their classroom work than they are to include speaking and listening experiences within an 'event'. This chapter ends with a review of speaking and listening in the natural classroom experience, within lessons. As a coordinator it is essential to know the possibilities and to practise them.

The expectations of the literacy hour demand that pupils will work in groups for a sustained short period during the lesson. Unless children are able to use some of the strategies listed here, there will be considerable organisational difficulties for the teacher in attending to one group while others engage in worthwhile tasks.

Using group work to develop speaking and listening

It seems obvious that the best way to develop speaking and listening skills in children is to give them a chance to speak and listen. If you are one member of a group of 30 and the opportunity is provided for speaking and listening the chances are that you do 29 times more listening than you do speaking, unless you haven't understood the social rules. If we reduce the number of people in the group, the chance to speak rises. If we reduce the number in the group to 2, 3 or 4 the opportunity to speak is about balanced with the expectation of listening. In a group of 2 we have a 50 per cent chance of speaking. In a group of 3 it's 33 and so on. That still means we have got to listen for three times as long as we speak, but most of us can cope with that. If you watch people when they are out socially in large groups they tend to split very quickly into 2s, 3s and 4s to have conversations. Even 5s split for considerable periods of time into smaller groups. This is because we need that balance between speaking and listening and the chance to express our ideas and thoughts. If this is the process in the real world, maybe we should make use of that in the classroom. Within lessons we need to give children the chance to speak in groups of varying size, not for extended periods, but for short periods of time so that they can express their ideas, plan and predict, share some thoughts and opinions and describe to each other what is happening. If we make group work an integral part of most lessons, then we are achieving a balance between whole class and group teaching which would satisfy the need for adaptability but give children the chance to actively take part in the lesson that is unfolding before them.

For many teachers there is an uncertainty about what group work is. Since the Plowden Report in the late 1960s primary classrooms have been organised in groups. Children are arranged in ability groups, mixed ability groups, friendship, social, task and gender groups. All the evidence is, though, that in the vast majority of primary classrooms, children sit in groups and work separately. They may sit around a table, looking sociable, sharing equipment, but there is little interaction about the curriculum because children are on their own work agenda. The groups are ways of batching the children, of gathering them for their short sessions with the teacher.

If we can see that group work involves children actually working together, then speaking and listening are the essential elements. Even within a class lesson therefore, on any subject of the curriculum, it is preferable to make use of grouping children in to smaller numbers to:

Talk about what has just been said

Simply stop within the explanation, an experiment, a story and give children the chance to talk through what has just happened without an agenda, without a test at the end of it, without the expectation there is going to be a class discussion. Give children the opportunity to clarify what is happening.

To seek examples

Children might sit in 2s to seek further examples of particular number patterns within mathematics or to find examples of when they have had similar experiences during religious education lessons or to think of examples of reptiles that live in certain conditions as a prelude to a class discussion. Working in 2s or 3s to seek examples before a class discussion helps to overcome the problem that many teachers have within class lessons of unwanted or incorrect examples being voiced by individuals which take the lesson off track. By talking in 2s beforehand, some of the incorrect examples are corrected by other children before they get voiced. Similarly the 'silly' offering which often creates chaos and takes concentration away from the larger group is lost when the person likely to offer it says it to another child and realises it's way off the target. It simply does not get used within the class discussion.

To admit misunderstandings

After an explanation by the teacher, or a demonstration, or a story in history or a set of instructions in geography about grid references, it is useful to stop and allow children to discuss with each other where they are having problems and what they do not understand. Sometimes the chance to do this stops children dropping out because they do not know what is going on or it removes the need for the teacher to run round to individual children trying to put the problem right. Other children simply help. Equally, a class discussion about common misunderstandings can help children come to terms with concepts, knowledge or skills quite quickly rather than become even more muddled as time goes on.

Getting groups to find some ideas

Being stuck for ideas is a real turn off for children. A blank piece of paper and a chance to come up with something riveting is likely to lead to poor behaviour and work avoidance, because to be unable to think of an idea is to be exposed. Children find all sorts of ways of avoiding having ideas. To sit in a 2 or 3 and to share some ideas or to feed off each other and come up with some thoughts is a way forward which would change the climate in the classroom. To get children with one sheet of paper, one pencil and three minds brainstorming why it might be that a certain phenomena appears in science or how we might build a certain structure, or how we might start to plan the next class assembly is a wonderful starting point for creative thought.

To feed off other people's ideas

If each group of three has produced some starting points to pass them on and ask other groups to add to the ideas, expand them, extend them, come up with a new slant is one way of generating enormous amounts of thoughts in a very quick time. Somewhere within all of this will be some real jewels which are worth exploring in-depth.

To pick out the important bits

As children go through Key Stage 2 they need to be able to prioritise and identify what really matters. So after a story, a video or assembly, to sit children in 2s and 3s and give them the opportunity to jot down the things that they thought were important, significant or really crucial is a worthwhile thing to do. For a start it gives the teacher an idea of what the children thought mattered and therefore whether the message really went home. Beyond this it is an opportunity for children to really contribute to class discussion, having had a few minutes to think about what needs to be said.

In all of these examples children are getting to grips with the curriculum subject, but are also having the opportunity to speak and listen for short but intense periods of time. On top of this, they are developing those social skills that are so important in terms of their overall development. The teacher is having the chance to really involve the children within the session and in many cases the session will move much more quickly for these brief five minute hyphens that give the children the chance to prepare some thoughts for their individual contributions to the class. In so many classes, class discussions are misnomers, few children take an active part, many children fail to contribute. They fail because they do not contribute and because they do not understand what is happening. They think their contribution will be inappropriate, they do not wish to look silly, they get bored, they can't get their words in, they are embarrassed, they cannot follow, one person takes the conversation off at an angle, certain children dominate.

Once the habit of talking in 2s and 3s within the course of a lesson is established, children become much more confident, much more able to contribute because they are contributing for their colleagues rather than simply standing alone. It is worth asking yourself, would you rather stand up and voice your opinion as an individual or would you prefer to check it out first with a couple of others and then speak for the three of you?

Taking opportunities to use small groups within the pattern of a larger lesson or a project is one method of developing speaking and listening skills within children. It is possible to use more structured forms of group work within lessons in most subjects once the children have understood how various patterns of groupwork operate.

In the early 1990s a national oracy project took place in a few LEAs around the country. Within this project, teachers tried to develop in their classrooms ways of helping children to work effectively in groups to extend learning. The project explored different arrangements for grouping so that information could be quickly understood, skills could be quickly learned and ideas could be quickly grasped (see Figure 6.1).

FIG 6.1
Approaches to group work

Brainstorm

quick collecting of ideas from
members of group — try
recording points on a spider
diagram or flow chart

Snowball

share ideas from individuals
to pairs to fours and finally
with whole class or group

Rainbow

all members of a group become
'envoys'. New groups are
formed to pool ideas and take
the discussion further. Groups
may be re-organised according
to numbers, colours etc.

Talk partners

Pairs talk to each other
regularly to evaluate, test out
ideas, explain, ask questions
etc.

Jigsaw

'Home' group members each take
responsibility for investigating a particular
aspect of the work. Re-group into 'Expert'
groups each focusing on one aspect. Later
return to 'Home' group where all
individuals piece together their findings

Role-play (or simulation)

Members of group in different
roles to explore an issue etc.
— useful for trying out new
voices, ideas, vocabulary —
and for empathy

Envoys

a messenger from one
group to another to report,
share ideas

Visitors

one person visits all groups in
turn to collect good ideas,
sharing with whole class later

All of these approaches to group work rely upon the notion
that children are expected to get on with each other and learn
from each other, rather than compete as individuals or as
groups within the class. Most schools have within their aims
that they wish children to be well behaved and helpful people.
Using group work in this way can ensure that such things
become a probability rather than a wish. If teachers can use
some of these techniques within the Literacy Hour they will be
more able to fulfil the expectations. Beyond that, across all the
subjects of the curriculum, the quality of one aspect of English
teaching will be considerably well developed.

Part three

Developing whole school policies and schemes of work

Chapter 7   Working on planning

One of the essentials of good teaching is planning. The planning, though, needs to inform and support the teaching rather than becoming an end in itself. For so many teachers planning is an activity that demands time, effort and paper but remains a clerical exercise to keep other people content as opposed to an activity that forms the foundation for effective teaching. The challenge for the English coordinator is to set up effective planning systems that are economic with time, help teachers to teach well, and ensure the best possible learning chances for children. It is often argued that the process of producing a planning framework is as important as the product. The process is important but most would agree that when it is sorted out it is a weight off the mind. Better to have it done and systems in operation with routine review than constantly working towards something that will be finished one day.

Where to start in English

If we start with some general statements about English we will be repeating some of the points argued elsewhere in this book, but any planning must start from policy and some statements need to be agreed:

- about the *nature* of English;
- about *issues* relating to English;

- about the *demands* of the National Curriculum and the expectations of the Literacy Strategy;
- about the *aims, activities and experiences* the school promotes.

Some clear policy direction is provided by the school that says, 'At Make Believe Primary School we recognise that the four components of English are interdependent and of equal importance'. It is this sort of policy statement about the nature of English that sets the direction for planning processes.

'Planning in English needs to address learning objectives first and content second,' is the sort of issue that the school needs to consider.

In terms of National Curriculum demands teachers need to look at the Programmes of Study in terms of writing, where children should experience ideas of developing, organising and communicating, writing as a source of enjoyment, and writing as a means of thinking and learning, as well as the grammar of standard written forms, such as nouns, prepositions and tenses.

These demands, though, are within the context of the Literacy Strategy which sets out the structure of a framework for the use of time and the expectations of what will be taught and when, both over a period of years and within the designated 'Literacy Hour'.

The school will decide the sorts of experiences it believes essential for its pupils. 'At Make Believe Primary School we encourage children to develop responsibility for themselves and others.' If this is an aim for the school, one way of addressing it is through learning in English and through effective interpretation of the literacy strategy.

These areas come together in the policy statement for the subject, including literacy, and in turn, they guide the planning process as it moves on to its next stage.

Do we need to bother now that we are being given a literacy strategy 'Framework for Teaching' in yet another ring binder?

Well, yes . . . but not so much as previously. There is absolutely no point in spending lots of time and energy reproducing something that mimics the literacy framework document. The document has been produced by people who have had time and have the expertise to do it for you. It tells you what to do, when to do it, how to do it. Cynics would say that it is so prescriptive that it tells you when to have a coffee or blow your nose!

What it does do, is to show a school how to meet the expected range of work over the seven primary years. It shows how the National Curriculum expectations for reading and writing can be accomplished in the time available and it sets an order. What it does not do is bring in the expected levels of speaking and listening coverage and, of course, there is no acknowledgment of the different circumstances or aims of different schools.

We should not, hopefully, expect to a lot of extra work beyond that which is provided, but it is sensible to look at ways we can plan the whole of the English curriculum, including but going beyond, the Framework for Literacy.

Scheming — getting it sorted out for four years

Providing the scheme of work is like deciding on the menu, given that you have the ingredients of the National Curriculum, the Literacy Framework, and the school's aims to hand.

The process is easy enough

- Identify learning objectives for each year. This builds in progression and continuity.
- Identify specific English focused units for each year group, linking learning objectives in speaking, listening, reading and writing. These are identified 'blocks' of work.
- Identify the objectives that can be taught through other subjects. These are the aspects that 'link'.
- Identify the objectives that should be part of the daily or weekly diet for children. This is the 'ongoing' work.
- Plan out the blocks and the links through the year groups.

When that is done, an outline scheme of work has been produced. It tells everyone who is to teach what and when it should be taught.

The Literacy Framework is, in effect, the 'ongoing work'. It goes on for an hour a day, the 'literacy hour', creating that gradual input of learning. In many schools in many subjects, this has been an area that has been weakly addressed. It has been assumed that teachers were teaching the 'basics' as children plodded through individualised text book and exercise schemes, or that all teachers were teaching the basics as and when they arose. Sadly in some classrooms they never arose, partly because children were working their way through often meaningless exercises and not meeting interesting approaches to learning about text!

The Literacy Framework can be lifted wholesale to your school scheme of work for English and become the section for 'ongoing' work. The blocked and the linked units of work in English still need to be planned to fit in with the National Curriculum expectations and to meet the aims of the school. As outlined in Part 1, there are differences in studying a text to learn about the author or the quality of writing, or about our responses, from the study of text to increase reading and writing skills (see Figure 7.1).

From the daily menu:
■ teacher reading aloud from a range of texts — poetry, novels, picture books, information books, newspapers;
■ children reading to each other — pairs, groups, whole class;
■ working in the writing area;
■ using the word processor;
■ using the library.

And from the weekly menu:
■ collaborative writing — producing books, newspapers, displays;
■ telling stories on tape;
■ children dictating captions for display;
■ group reading and discussion of sets of books;
■ and anything else from the trolley.

English Scheme of Work Medium-Term Plan

This offers general guidance to colleagues about how to approach a focus most effectively.

At this stage teachers plan for assessment, making sure criteria for success are clearly outlined and shared. A variety of assessment opportunities should be planned for over a range of activities during the key stage.

Learning objectives are set in terms of what the children will be able to do, know and understand, drawn from long-term plan.

The plan sequences the activities to provide points to the short-term plan.

The plan will form a dynamic resource base with the variety of focuses over the year and over the key stage.

The plan must reflect the interrelated aspects of English.

Example

Scheme of work (medium-term plan)

Year/Class _____

From _____ To _____

Plan for: En Ma Sci DT IT Hi Ge Ar Mu PE RE

Cross curricular themes / dimensions _____

CONTENT / OBJECTIVES	ACTIVITIES TO BE UNDERTAKEN	ASSESSMENT	ESTIMATED TIME
Enter: ■ learning objectives from the scheme of work (long-term plan) ■ further details appropriate to pupils being taught	Include: ■ main activities ■ resource requirements ■ strategies for differentiation	Indicate how the objectives will be assessed i.e. ■ discussions with pupils ■ observation of pupils ■ marking pupil's work ■ informal or formal tests	In terms of sessions or hours

FOCUS ON YEAR GROUP

Responsibility: Class Teacher(s) with support from subject and / or year group coordinator

FIG 7.1
Medium term plan

To offer further help a scheme can include some checks on progression, such as

- skills to be developed and extended
- texts to be used
- suggested activities or experiences
- assessment strategies to be used
- expected teaching approaches to be used
- lists of resources, where to find them, and whom to consult
- types of evaluation needed to inform future planning.

English Menu

Sample for Key Stage 2

	Autumn		Spring		Summer	
	English focus units	English through other subjects	English focus units	English through other subjects	English focus units	English through other subjects
Year 3	Novel as a theme *Ten in a Bed* by Janet and Allan Ahlberg	Romans (history) ■ jigsaw technique for info. research ■ empathetic writing	Poetry — light verse	Food (science) ■ leaflets ■ accounts ■ charts ■ descriptions ■ poems	Folk tales	St Lucia (geography) ■ descriptions (brochures) ■ Caribbean poetry ■ captions for photos ■ postcards/letters
Year 4	Poetry — modern poetry	Ancient Egypt (history) ■ report writing ■ descriptions ■ info. retrieval	Newspapers	Habitats (science) ■ notes ■ different ways of presenting information ■ labelling	Novel as a theme *Conker* by Michael Morpurgo	Local Area (geography) ■ make info. booklets ■ posters ■ brochures ■ directions ■ surveys
Year 5	Letter writing	Tudors (history) ■ biographies ■ writing in role ■ diaries, letters	Novel as a theme *Bill's New Frock*, Anne Fine	Look After Yourself (science) ■ posters ■ charts ■ instructions	Poetry — 'Pied Piper'	Environmental Issues (geography) ■ debate ■ present argument ■ persuasive writing ■ letter writing ■ poems
Year 6	Novel as a theme *Carrie's War* by Nina Bawden	Britain since 1930 (history) ■ interviews ■ diaries ■ newspaper reports	Poetry — story poems, ballads, pre-20th century	Electricity (science) ■ posters ■ leaflets ■ news reports ■ bills!	Myths and legends	Europe (geography) ■ debate ■ present info. in different formats ■ accounts ■ research and compile info.

FIG 7.2
English menu plan

The scheme does not have to be extensive, it has to be easily interpreted. The sample shown below offers a teacher a clear picture of what needs to be covered in her class in a particular year. It provides a guide, but it ensures coverage, it addresses progression and it suggests content (Figure 7.2).

Planning in more detail

As the planning moves on then each teacher needs to consider more detail, perhaps with the support of the coordinator. Taking items from the scheme for the year, the teacher decides on the actual recipe, the amounts, the cooking times and the best preparation. A pro-forma can help and this can be organised to help take the blocked and linked units into detail.

Within the Literacy Framework there are pro-formas for termly and half termly planning for the 'ongoing' Literacy Hour. Given the range of work identified, the teacher has to structure the use of time to ensure content is addressed in the time available. The balance of this time varies according to the timing of Easter, the phases of the moon, and the need for various elections in some schools.

A similar approach needs to be adopted for the linked and blocked units to give coherence to the overall package offered to the children.

Planning for tomorrow

This is where the waiter writes on his pad so that he does not forget anything; it is the teacher's short-term planning, the day by day notes, ideas, 'don't forgets' that teachers need to make. We can use postcards, a note pad, a professional diary, a school pro-forma or even our heads, but people worry about using those these days in case they are asked for evidence.

This is the section in the Literacy Framework which outlines the hour. It is still left to the teacher to take items from the 'what' and put them in order to create the hour. Maybe in time the prescription will become even more specific and there will be the hour by hour formula. The problem at the time of producing the framework is that the point is reached where it is recognised that no one recipe will fit every situation. The small two–teacher school with four year groups in a class will need a different pattern from the large urban school with scope for mixing and setting children.

A few jottings might be all that is needed to remember key points in a session but more and more schools are using pro-formas. The important element at this stage is the preparation of materials, the thinking through of key questions, and the clear idea of how groups will be organised. Sometimes we are in danger of writing too much and thinking too little. Planning should almost be the writing process in reverse. We start with lots of detail, the finished article and gradually come down to notes and jottings to remind us as necessary. At the stage of running the classroom and the English lesson, teachers need to use the planning that makes it easier for them to work; not systems and techniques to help the coordinator, the head, or an inspector who may appear in four years' time. As long as the right meal gets to the right table does it matter how the order was written down?

Showing teachers how to involve children in planning

Planning for effective learning goes well beyond producing charts, lists, notes and folders in order to show 'powers that be' that we are doing our planning. It goes further than producing documentation to pull content together into a coherent order and working out the best way to present it. Planning is about being clear about what we are trying to do and being clear about how to achieve it — before we set off. It is about thinking ahead and charting a course so that we are more likely to succeed and avoid pitfalls on the way.

As has been said, most schools do not teach English in isolation. We teach English to help fulfil the aims of the school. Most school aims contain ideals such as trying to help the children become 'confident' or 'responsible' or 'able to make decisions'. These personal qualities and characteristics can only be developed in terms of lessons, events or routines which take place in the school; they need a context and one of the contexts is English lessons.

During inspection, teachers are aware that their lessons are graded, in part, in terms of the pupils' response. Many think this is to do with behaviour and if the children work hard, quietly, and apply themselves to the task set, then the grade will be good. In order to achieve this many teachers play safe and give the children very simple, basic things to do with very little room for error. The reality is that, for response to be recognised as good, the children need to be seen to offer appropriate responses. They need to show that they have positive attitudes to learning, that they are well developed socially, and that they behave well. All this goes forward to a section about the school's standards achieved, under attitudes, behaviour and personal development. If we want to do well in this aspect then we must set the children tasks which will help them to show how they can work, as well as what they can achieve. By setting tasks which involve children we will be more likely to address the aims of the school within lessons.

If this concept can be established with teachers, they may need help in making the connection with what we actually do to help it to happen. We cannot really instruct the children in being 'more responsible', we cannot just demonstrate 'being confident', and we cannot help children to 'learn to use their ideas' unless we give them the chance to do it. So, within English how might we help teachers to see ways of involving the children? As an example, we can look at the use of information texts to address a planned topic, an example of 'linked' work, and explore how it would work in the classroom.

The Literacy Framework includes many examples of using information texts. In Year 5, term 3, the text level work is on reading comprehension and writing composition and includes elements of investigation and analysis of arguments as well as constructing full texts to persuade others. There is, though, no expectation set in terms of the content and it is for the teacher to decide to what extent this should take place within the Literacy Hour or in other lessons, for example, in history. Further exploration will help teachers with their planning.

Using information texts to address a planned topic

As with literature there are two elements which lie at the heart of work with children:

1   responding to the texts — being fascinated by the content and making sense of it in terms of one's previous knowledge;

2   learning how the texts work and how they require to be read.

The establishment of a pattern whenever these materials are being used, to provide information on a particular topic, will ensure these two elements are always addressed. Certain teaching strategies are important and have been described in numerous books and reports over the past twenty or more years. Whatever activities are planned in order to help children comprehend and use such materials (still often referred to as DARTS — Directed Activities Related To Texts) their use 'for real' in the classroom will work best when children are actively interested in and enthusiastic about what they are reading. We must not forget this in our desire to establish the efficient use of reading skills through such work.

The following pattern is useful in that it provides a common focus for whole class collaboration with a particular aim in mind — that of 'producing information' for others to appreciate.

---

1   Agree the end product

In adult life we always have the form the work will take clear in our minds whenever we are 'producing information'. We might be writing a book or a newspaper article, creating a CD ROM, responsible for putting up a display or staging an exhibition, producing a television or radio programme or even directing a film. Knowing what we are aiming at helps to focus our work and to organise what we are trying to say. Throughout the process of gathering and sorting information we find ourselves mentally referring to and picturing the final production. The form provides a scaffold for the work.

This means that we should agree a form for the completed work before any work begins. If the scheme of work is 'The Second World War' perhaps the aim will be to produce a series of booklets each covering a particular aspect of the war years. Alternatively, we could be going to convert the classroom into an exhibition covering the topic. With a class of children such a focus also enables everyone to be working together towards the same end. Whether a child carries out her own work individually or in a two or three, they are also contributing to a whole class production.

---

2 Set a deadline

Deadlines really do help to focus thinking and aid concentration. So, four weeks today our exhibition will open or our booklets will be 'published'. Of course with young children it is not enough to set the deadline and expect them to be able to keep to it. So many topics in primary schools in the past have begun in a blaze of glory only to fizzle out, sometimes unfinished at the end of term. Timetables need to be constructed:

There need to be regular updates of work in progress with consideration of problems which might have arisen and ways of overcoming them.

3 Decide on the audience

Writers, film makers, television producers, CD ROM creators and exhibition directors always have a particular type of 'audience' in mind. Who is going to read the booklets? Who will come to our exhibition? How will this influence what we produce?

The above three decisions need to be made before any work begins. Together they provide **purpose** to the work and **pace** to its execution. In the children's eyes they are not just 'learning about' the Second World War, they are actively engaged in creating something concrete. In a sense the decisions are not about 'reading for information' at all, but about good primary practice. In addition though, the use of any reading material is always bound up with the attitude of the reader — whether it is a poem or an encyclopaedia. If we want children to use newspapers or information books efficiently and enthusiastically the provision of a definite aim to the work can make all the difference.

We are not, though, just aiming at enthusiasm. Now two important parts of the process of reading for information have to be addressed if we want children to engage with texts in a focused, efficient way.

Establish what the children already know

Before seeking out new information about the Second World War the class ought to pool its existing knowledge. This can be done through small groups 'brainstorming' on large sheets of paper — anything anyone thinks they know. In a brainstorm all contributions are accepted — there should be no discussion — so only minutes are required. Rather than use the sheets for discussion **before** the work it is a good idea simply to have some volunteers produce a master sheet which is then displayed throughout the next few weeks. As children gather information, items on the sheet will either be confirmed or proved to be mistaken. This can be indicated on the sheet and form the basis for regular discussion.

All new learning makes sense in terms of what we already know or think we know. Our previous knowledge might turn out to be right or wrong but the process of finding out means we actively engage with the texts which will tell us.

Decide what information is to be gathered

This should be the point at which information books or a CD ROM are first used. Children (just like adults!) require time to browse through texts in order to begin to sort out exactly what the topic in question is all about. Chapter headings in some books on the Second World War can be discussed to see if they cover the same aspects. While children are browsing or discussing, the teacher needs to remember that a major aim is to be a role model in terms of responding enthusiastically to the content. Our own demonstration of interest, our own sense of wonder, will prove to be infectious. From such an exercise a list can be drawn up which the class will use as the basis of the work. From the list questions need to be constructed so that children will approach any reading materials with something specific to find out. They are looking for answers now rather than just looking.

Now the work can begin. As coordinator you will be ensuring that children have access to a wide variety of sources in order to answer their questions. In terms of written materials there will be work on how to use them efficiently, sometimes as a separate exercise, sometimes as children are in the process of using them. Always the latter if at all possible!

Celebrate the product

As the deadline draws near so a sense of excitement and even a little anxiety should be felt in the classroom. Just as in 'real life'! When the final production, be it an exhibition or booklets or whatever, is finally ready the children need to be encouraged to talk with the 'audience' about the interesting aspects of the topic which they have learned. Just as we have shared our enthusiasm with them so they ought to share their enthusiasm with others. Young children should not feel reticent about pointing out and commenting on something which interested them. They will not just be taking the booklets home for mum or dad to read but in order to chat about the topic which they have covered.

Reflect on what has been learned

There are four elements which ought to be reviewed as the final part of the process:

■ the subject matter — interesting things we have learned about the Second World War;

■ the quality of the final product — what we think of our exhibition;

■ the ways of working — contributions/tensions in the groups and/or the class;

■ the reading and writing lessons — what we have learned about using information materials efficiently and effectively.

The work is then properly 'finished', with a recognisable conclusion. The last two elements can be reviewed so as to produce posters or prompt sheets for use in the future when the same skills and awareness will be required.

Chapter 8

Putting policy into practice

Introduction

Good subject understanding leads to the development of a set
of principles for teaching English but, using reading as an
example here, getting teachers to adopt the practices and make
them work is one of the real challenges facing the coordinator.

If we want to develop a *working* approach to the subject it is
important to follow a set of steps that take us from the
establishment of principles through to agreed approaches,
procedures and systems so that everybody in school is trying
to work in the same way. This is what is called a whole-school
approach. It is the approach in action that matters rather than
the written policy documents that are followed in a haphazard
way.

Establishing principles

If a school has a set of *aims* which have already been
established they can serve as a set of principles to guide the
way in which the teaching and learning will take place in a
school. Whether we are a coordinator for English, history, art,
IT or any other subject, the work of the subject should address
the overall aims for teaching and learning and the development
of a child in the fullest sense. These aspects of curriculum

leadership are referred to by the Teacher Training Agency within their expectations for the role.

Most primary schools have very similar aims and it is possible to take one of them as an example with which most schools will identify.

> The activities of the school should promote the development of the child's lively, enquiring mind.

This sort of aim, with some variation, would feature in the vast majority of schools. Most primary teachers, indeed most parents, would find some accord with such an aim. Whilst this is fine in principle and will be readily agreed and therefore established, the practice which goes forward to make this principle work is sometimes less secure. What matters is that we agree the practices that will make a difference.

Agreed practices

Without concentrating on English or any other subject we could list a series of practices which would try to address the principle of promoting a child's lively and enquiring mind. We could have such things as:

- inter-active displays;
- a school council;
- well-planned lessons;
- visits to places of interest;
- artefacts around the classroom.

All of these and many more are valid but for the purposes of looking at the contribution English can make to the same we could focus on one example which relates to the

> effective use of the library provision

If children are to develop a lively, enquiring mind then it is essential that they are able to use the library effectively. Some children will be able to manage well but some will have difficulties and therefore we need to identify some of *the issues and problems.*

Issues and problems

Staff could brainstorm the issues and problems connected with the use of the school library. Most teachers will identify with the difference between the rhetoric and reality of setting up a library that can be used easily by the pupils. Although the issues may be different in most schools it is possible for teachers to identify with those in the case study below.

> **Our library**
> - The library is separate from the rest of the school.
> - The library is not an easy space to organise.
> - The library shelving is relatively high for small children.
> - Much of the stock is older.
> - There is a significant amount of new books.
> - The room is relatively unattractive being one of the areas to be sorted out fairly soon.
> - The library is used as a gathering place for television etc.
> - Children are generally taken there as classes.
> - Children are rarely allowed there as individuals.

These are a series of issues and problems, some of which are positive, some of which are negative. It is possible to look at the list and identify with the challenges that the teachers face. In some schools the problems are recognised and the difficulties accepted and therefore we almost take it as read that the aim of trying to encourage children to have enquiring minds is not a real possibility, given the problems we face. It is possible to move further along by *looking for the reasons* that lie behind some of the issues and problems being experienced. So, in terms of the case study library above, we might identify some of the reasons as:

> - the accommodation is on a 'needs must' basis, to create the best provision elsewhere in the school;
> - in the summer the library is a cooler area in which to take children;
> - a dedicated space is at least provided for the library;
> - improving stock takes time due to previous significant neglect.

People can offer many reasons for the occurrence of issues and problems and usually they are valid. The challenge facing the coordinator is to try to move forward from the current situation rather than simply accept that aims and principles cannot be met.

Therefore, it is important that we devise some *strategies* which will help overcome the challenges associated with effective use of library provision.

Some strategies

- There could be time devoted on a closure day for the whole staff team working to sort it out because all the staff need to be aware of how the library is organised.
- The shelving could be moved to allow a whole class to gather comfortably towards one end of the library for television and story.
- Plants, curtaining and drapes could be put into the library to create a more comfortable feel.
- Displays of children's work particularly related to books could be established.
- There needs to be a set system for the cataloguing, storage and retrieval of books.
- Guidelines on how to use the library could be displayed on a notice board.
- Systems need to be established to enable children to use the library effectively.

Many of these strategies are relatively easy to carry out, but they need that precious commodity — time. Time is available in schools but often it slips by without being fully utilised. Every school has five days a year devoted to staff training for curriculum development. If all the staff spend the day working on something like the school library the result should be:

- an understanding of expectations;
- a feeling of achievement;
- a wish to make it work so the day is not wasted.

By using a closure day in this way, significant steps forward can be taken, and some of the more instant strategies adopted. Others such as teaching children how to use a library effectively take more time.

It is not only the structuring of the environment that will make the library work and therefore achieve the aims, it is necessary to support and teach the children in the ways in which the library can operate. We need to offer *guidance and suggestions*.

Guidance and suggestions

- When a child removes a book from the library shelf a 'paddle' the size of a table tennis bat made from cardboard could be inserted from where the book was removed. As children bring books back they are able to see where a book might fit. They then have to check whether the book is in the right section.

- Individual children can be allowed to use the library when they have succeeded in gaining a library licence. They will be taught to use a library effectively, to use a catalogue system to find a book. They will be taught how to use the library respectfully and they will be taught to return books to the correct place. When they feel they understand the work of the library, they will enter a test and if successful on the appointed day will be issued with a school library user's licence. This licence would allow them to use the library unsupervised on the clear understanding that they behave in certain expected ways.

Library Licence

This library licence has been awarded to

....

for demonstrating an ability to:

- follow our library code;
- know and use the Dewey Classification System to select and replace books;
- work quietly and cooperatively with others in the library;
- keep the library tidy and in good order;
- know what to do if you have a problem.

Congratulations.

Examples of guidance and suggestions such as this and agreement by the staff as to a willingness to trial things is an important part of the process of taking principles into practice.

Once staff agree to trial things they are *piloting and trialing techniques.*

The techniques that have been agreed need to be tried by all the staff in order to see whether they work and to iron out any problems. Problems are then referred back to the issues and problem section and the loop begins again. However, when a technique works effectively it moves forward and becomes an agreed approach, procedure or system.

In the example of the case study school, the suggestion of offering the library licence has worked very well. A classroom assistant has taught the children the library systems using a structured approach with exercises built in to short teaching periods with small groups during the week. Examples of some of the exercises are shown below and on p. 112.

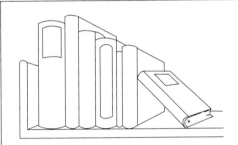

The books in a library are divided into two sections, fiction and non-fiction.

Fiction books are stories made up by the author.

Non-fiction books are based on facts and give us information.

Look at a pile of books and see if you can decide if they are fiction or non-fiction.

Which books did you find?

Author	Title	Fiction or Non-fiction

A B C D E F G H I J K L M
N O P Q R S T U V W X Y Z

This is the order of the alphabet. In libraries, fiction books are arranged in order of the author's surname.

Put the names of these authors into alphabetical order.

Remember — use the surname.

Eric <u>Hill</u>	1. _____
Jules <u>Verne</u>	2. _____
Beatrix <u>Potter</u>	3. _____
Roald <u>Dahl</u>	4. _____
Maurice <u>Sendak</u>	5. _____
Helen <u>Oxenbury</u>	6. _____
Kenneth <u>Grahame</u>	7. _____
Raymond <u>Briggs</u>	8. _____
Edward <u>Lear</u>	9. _____
Allan <u>Ahlberg</u>	10. _____

ENCYCLOPAEDIA

Here is a picture of a set of Encyclopaedia. It is called ....
There are .... volumes in this set.

VOL 1	VOL 2	VOL 3	VOL 4	VOL 5	VOL 6	VOL 7	VOL 8	VOL 9	VOL 10
The School Encyclopaedia	The School Encyclopaedia	The School Encyclopaedia	The School Encyclopaedia	The School Encyclopaedia	The School Encyclopaedia	The School Encyclopaedia	The School Encyclopaedia	The School Encyclopaedia	The School Encyclopaedia
P-Q-R	C-D	E-F-G	H-I-J	K-L-M	N-O	P-Q-R	S-T-U	V-W	X-Y-Z

In which volume will you find information about:

1. Ladybirds ....
2. Television ....
3. Roald Dahl ....
4. Elephants ....
5. Romans ....
6. New Zealand ....

When the children feel they understand how to use the library and are confident that they can do it, they complete a form and enter for the test. A different classroom assistant sends them their date of appointment, and on the day gives them a test. Children have to find two books that contain information on, say, Egypt. They are given books and asked where they would fit them back on the shelving, including perhaps an outsized book that goes somewhere different. They are observed as they work through the catalogue system to find an appropriate book. They are expected to use the index of the book to find the location of information and they need to be able to identify the author, publisher and date of different publications within the library.

There is then a series of 'highway code' type questions about the use of the library, such as

■ 'What would you do if you came into the library and found a book on the floor?'
■ 'What would you do if you came into the library and found a plant knocked down?'

- ■ 'What would you do if you came into the library and saw some younger children being silly?'
- ■ 'What would you do if you came into the library and found an older child being silly?'

If the child is successful, they are told that they qualify for a licence and when they receive it, the licence then enables them to go to the library, with teacher's permission, without adult supervision. They can also take with them a friend who has not yet qualified for a licence on the same principle as a driver with a licence can supervise a learner.

As such a technique becomes accepted through pilot or trial procedures, the school moves towards *an agreed approach, procedure, system* and therefore, since everybody is taking part, the school has a *policy*.

This policy can then be written down and communicated to all staff, parents and children and becomes part of the working of the school. In this way the principle is seen as part of the working life of children and teachers rather than rhetoric which rarely meets reality. When this is happening the school is operating a policy.

By reviewing policy and practice and devising suggestions to address real issues, it is possible to avoid practice being seen as 'gimmicks'. The library examples are the practical solutions to policy issues in the school. They are not just 'good ideas', 'new ways of working', 'tips for teachers'. The process of policy review clarifies intentions.

Developing a policy is a long-term business but significant progress can be made quickly because the policy draws together aspects of the school which are being developed in various places. The teaching and learning policy becomes a central strand of development with the school and brings a coherence to various developments. The English coordinator would seek to generate practices within the subject which should enhance the possibility of achieving the principle aims of the school. Equally the English coordinator would be supporting other colleagues in other subjects through the piloting and trialing of techniques suggested by them.

In many schools there is an enormous gap between the rhetoric and the reality. This is because the practices that are agreed fail to come into action. Often this is the fault of no-one. It is not a set of negative actions that cause a policy to fail. More often it is a series of consequences which result from issues and problems that have not been foreseen or which are not addressed when they first arise. This is why many policies flounder at a very early stage.

By working through the stages identified within this section, it should be possible to ensure that agreed practices become reality in terms of the working procedures, approaches and systems within classrooms and therefore address the established principles. This approach, of working through the series of steps, can take place for any aspect of any subject, or any area of work within the school. It helps to get frustrations and concerns out in the open and keep people working positively forward in order to achieve the things the school thinks are important.

Chapter 9 — Producing a development plan

In order that the coordinator can encourage colleagues to develop practice that matches policy it is useful to produce a development plan for English — a step by step route towards good practice, effective teaching, and raised standards. This can be addressed in smaller bites, looking at different aspects of the subject at different times, gradually building the overall plan. An example of how this might work within the area of poetry is offered here to illustrate the process essential to development planning.

Begin with an audit

The starting point for producing a development plan is an 'audit' of the present work of the school in English. It could be that the school has recently received an inspection report from OFSTED. This is an example of an audit.

The school has to produce a plan of how it will respond to the key issues for action. If there are issues for English, the audit is already done and the action points already identified, all that remains is to produce the plan.

Even if the key issues do not refer directly to English there may be starting points which can be addressed in part through work in English. For example, it could be that the OFSTED report has highlighted key issues for action which emphasise the need to develop a wider use of teaching styles across the curriculum. This will almost certainly involve the examination of ways in which more effective English teaching can support other subjects. Again it may be that there is a key issue which emphasises the extension of more able children and it is through English, in part, that a more realistic provision can be managed.

If there has not been an inspection, then the subject leader needs to do a small scale audit to look at where the school's aims and principles are being met. If the coordinator is able to audit aspects of the school work in English, the prospect of inspection is not so threatening, the coordinator is prepared; there will be no surprises. The coordinator is confident, knowing what is happening in the subject and can show inspectors evidence of the work done. The audit will show what needs to be done and the development that results will show a realistic picture of how this will be achieved.

The word 'audit' carries connotations of business and commerce, but it is no bad thing for schools to ask themselves how well they are performing. However, any audit needs to be manageable, kept in proportion and used to shed some light upon what is and is not being achieved.

Many teachers find simple pro-formas useful and effective. A pro-forma guides thinking and acts as a notepad, but its very size limits the amount of writing and stops the process becoming too cumbersome.

Three useful aspects of provision can be useful starting points for audit:
1   the learning experiences of children;
2   the learning environment;
3   the resources.

By looking at these areas in some detail it will be possible to highlight how well the school is performing in many areas of the curriculum without over-complicating the work to be done. The pro-forma can be used as a vehicle for encouraging the collection of evidence to work through the process of thinking about development. The starting point is to identify some aspects of each focus and try to decide what represents good practice. In English it is perhaps more appropriate to begin with reading, writing, speaking and listening or Standard English and concentrate the audit on one of these key features rather than try to do everything at once. The collection of evidence would be more effective if more people in school were involved or at least were aware of the initiative taking place. The example below is a picture of the process with regard to pupil learning experiences specifically in terms of the use of poetry.

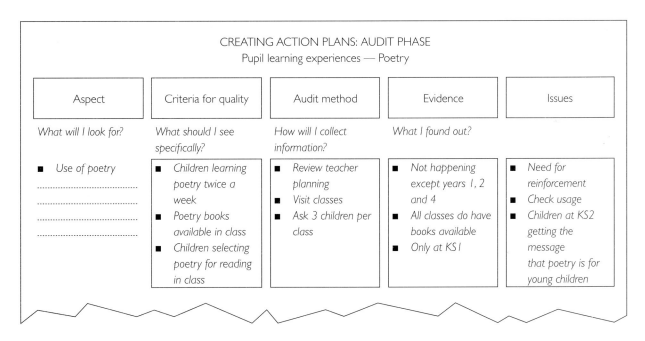

FIG 9.1
Pupil learning experiences
— poetry

By working with very precise questions, such as:

- what would I look for?

- what should I see?

- how will I collect information?

- what have I found out?

it is possible to reach a point where issues can be clearly identified.

Other staff will be more receptive and more committed to any development if they can see that the issues identified arise from some proper analysis rather than whims and fancy on the part of the coordinator. The fact that some monitoring has been taking place will have heightened awareness that the aspect is being considered and people will be prepared to move forward.

Following an audit it is possible to:

Create a development plan . . . use of poetry

Having used the audit to highlight the issues we can go on from there.

Action
If children at Key Stage 2 are getting the idea that poetry is not for them, what can be done about it?
- Buy better text books.
- Insist that all teachers lead a poetry session once a week.
- Feature poetry in assembly.
- Make choral speaking an important regular activity.

Identify responsibility
- Who is involved? All teachers . . .
- Who is checking it is happening? Key Stage team leader, headteacher . . .

Set a timescale
- When should progress be apparent? By half term.

How will we know it's worked? what are the success criteria?
- Repeat the audit and examine results.
- Check teacher planning.
- Ask children's views.

Provide resources
- Buy better stock.
- Use the local library service.
- Move current stock around the classrooms in school.

Envisage problems
- What about the reluctant teacher who hates poetry?
- How do we avoid the 'pop' poetry taking over?
- What about classes where discipline is not so strong — choral speaking?
- How will everyone find time?

This last section is an important element of development planning. So many people do lovely plans without thinking about the problems. It is as though they hope they will not happen. No amount of paperwork will overcome the problems associated with making things happen; getting action. You get action by taking action. We do this in practical ways described elsewhere. The documentation can only support, it must not be a burden. It must help to develop the learning and achievements of pupils.

Having audited a range of aspects of the teaching of English, including perhaps the effectiveness of the Literacy Hour, it should be possible to put together an overall development plan for English.

Producing a development plan for English

Organising a development plan for English need not be a daunting challenge. The plan is a structure to help guide and justify the actions to be taken within the development of the subject. If it is integrated with the development plans from other subjects there is an overall plan which fits together to provide the overall route map for curriculum development for some time ahead. With such plans in place the school should move forward, confident that everyone knows what is happening, when, and can anticipate success.

The first stage of producing a plan is to think through where development needs to occur in the next year. The spur for this can come through audits of curriculum provision to check against what is expected within the National Curriculum, analysis of assessment results to reveal what is needing to be addressed or extended, using an OFSTED report to identify strengths and weaknesses within the subject, or asking teachers, children or parents what might be areas of concern for future development.

If we know what the areas of concern are, then we need to know what we are going to do about them. In essence, we are listing the jobs to be done. Then we need to sort out the order of the list so that it is manageable. We need to make sure we know what we are trying to achieve and when the deadline for finishing will be. If there are any costs then that will affect things and we need to decide how we will check that what we do is working. Like so many developments in education, the job of producing a development plan is one which has become over-complex and stressful, full of terminology management speak, when in fact the job is a fairly simple task of decision making and recording a common sense approach to the next phase of the task.

Producing the development plan can be traced step by step by following the thinking through and constructing notes for possible inclusion in the plan. An example for some aspects of literacy is shown to illustrate the outline planning which needs to take place (see Figure 9.2).

Given this preliminary thinking, the coordinator for English can work with the other coordinators, to build up the development plan for the whole school. It is a case of setting priorities across the school, of argument, compromise, give and take, and finally agreeing what needs to be done and what will have to wait.

Figures 9.2 and 9.3 are extracts from a primary school development plan for English. They show clearly what needs to be done (issue), how it will be done (action), what is expected afterwards (success), when it will be done (date), what it will cost (resources), how the school will know if it is being done successfully (monitoring), and what INSET is needed (requirements). The figures also identify which of the overall aims these issues relate to and give a coherence and justification for actions within school which makes them both difficult to argue against and help to determine priorities.

The idea of the Subject Development Plan is that it should guide the work of the coordinator and fit that work into the overall plan for the school. It should be open to everyone to allow the coordinator to provide a route for everyone so that requests for action and changes of practice are understood. It needs to be concise, readable and easily interpreted. It needs to be read and referred to often; not produced and filed until next time. It is a working document and it needs to be made to work.

PRIMARY SCHOOL — SCHOOL DEVELOPMENT PLAN
MANAGEMENT / SUBJECT — TARGET SETTING

Management/Subject area: ..English.......

Coordinator: ....

Issue for development	Action to be taken	Success criteria	Date for completion	Resource/cost implications	Monitoring strategies	INSET requirements	Priority
Writing — Specific writing categories targeted on 7 year plan for each year group? Handwriting — Jarman — others to supplement special needs and aid transition from print to cursive. Spelling — Stages to be followed rigorously.	To work closely with JS throughout summer and autumn term '97 and follow up any initiatives stated by him. Also to amend and then monitor the existing English policy to make it more relevant and effective in KPS.	To raise standards throughout school especially at end of key stages with immediate reference to NC SATs, i.e. more children with good Level 2's at Y2 and more children with Level 4 and Level 5 at Y6.	March	12 Literacy INSET sessions with JS already costed.	Snapshots. Collections of specified samples of work. A3 Sheet SATs results.	Literacy sessions During Summer and Autumn Term	

FIG 9.2
Example of outline planning

Primary School — School development plan

Development area: CURRICULUM 4							
Issue for development	Action to be taken	Success criteria	Date for completion	Resource / cost implications	Monitoring strategies	INSET requirements	Sch Aim
C16. Support staff development on Reading. **LINK: R9/R26/R27/ A3/S3**	Discuss the most appropriate means and system of support with Head and English Adviser, in relation to INSET programme taking place.	Teaching of reading is developed systematically and consistently across the school in order to raise standards of achievement in reading.	Sept to Sept	£4,000 from book fund to support the development of reading skills.	Measurable progress by all children in reading abilities as measured by SATs and NFER tests.	Literacy sessions during Summer and Autumn Terms.	4
C17. Writing — Specific writing categories targeted on 7 year plan for each year group.	To work closely with English Adviser throughout Summer and Autumn terms and follow up any initiatives started.	To raise writing standards throughout school especially at end of key stages with intermediate reference to NC, SATs, (more children with good Level 2 at Y2 and more children with Level 4 and Level 5 at Y6).	Mar	12 Literacy INSET sessions with JS £2,500 from GEST I	Snapshots. Collections of specified samples of work. A3 Sheet SATs results.	Literacy sessions during Summer and Autumn Terms.	4
C18. Handwriting — Jarman and others to supplement special needs and aid transition from print to cursive.	Amend and then monitor the existing English policy to make it more relevant and effective in our school.	To raise the standard of handwriting across both key stages.	Mar	12 Literacy INSET sessions with JS £2,500 from GEST I	Snapshots. Collections of specified samples of work. A3 Sheet SATs results.	Literacy sessions during Summer and Autumn Terms.	4
C19. Spelling — Stages to be followed rigorously.	Class teachers to follow the agreed stages as identified in the policy document.	An improvement in the standard of spelling across both key stages.	May	12 Literacy INSET sessions with Jerry Swaine £2,500 from GEST I	Snapshots. Collections of specified samples of work. A3 Sheet SATs results.	Literacy sessions during Summer and Autumn Terms.	4

FIG 9.3
Example of a school development plan

Chapter 10

What about documentation? A summary of expectations

The spectre of OFSTED inspections has led many schools towards extensive documentation. Policy papers of all descriptions can be found in schools, but it is short sighted and naive to think that paper work is the key. It does not matter what the documents in the filing cabinet say, it is the practice in the classroom that is the real policy. If the two are in accord then that is fine, but the documents need to support the practice not stand in isolation.

It is essential that the coordinator takes on the task of trying to pull together the practice in the school and, as in this book, the documentation issues would eventually emerge as part of the job. Start with the practical things, the work in your own and other classrooms, use assembly, put up displays, lead enjoyable INSET sessions and as time goes along, begin the process of developing the paper work (see Figure 10.1).

So, what paper work would help to develop English in the school?

A policy statement:
- states some principles for the teaching of English in the school;
- states the agreed aim;
- states what the school expects the learners of English to be like as they leave the school;
- states how English should be taught;
- describes the assessment and record keeping procedures;
- will be based on the Programmes of Study for National Curriculum English;

- describes how adults will be involved;
- is short.

A scheme of work:
- describes how the policy is delivered in practice;
- offers guidance to teachers;
- puts content into order;
- explains what materials will be used;
- explains how resources are organised;
- defines which techniques will be used for what purposes with which children;
- defines the approaches for children with special needs;
- is detailed or it tells people where to turn to for advice.

A development plan or action plan:
- gives a clear picture of the stage of development of English at a given point in time; a curriculum statement;
- is part of the school development plan or post-inspection action plan;
- states what is planned for the subject of English in the near future, and in the longer term;
- defines proposed actions;
- establishes expectations or success criteria;
- states who is responsible;
- sets a time scale;
- identifies resource needs;
- is concise; it needs to fit with all the others from different subjects.

A booklet for parents:
- helps the parents to see how they can support their children's development in English;
- is written in friendly, jargon-free language;
- gives examples of how learning usually takes place;
- shows parents where there can sometimes be problems.

Staff guidelines:
- provide ideas and starting points;
- offer examples of planning; (see Figure 10.2)
- give sample lessons;
- list resources;
- contain examples of children's work;
- offer plans for displays;
- suggest useful educational visits;
- contain book lists for teachers;
- keep changing.

Assessment and recording portfolio:
- guides school understanding on assessment and recording;
- contains exemplars at each level;
- offers advice on recording methods;
- suggests 'what then';
- is relevant.

DOCUMENTATION FOR A SUBJECT

A DEVELOPMENT PLAN OR ACTION PLAN

- gives a clear picture of the stage of development of English at a given point in time; a curriculum statement is part of the school development plan or post inspection action plan
- states what is planned for the subject of English in the near future, and in the longer term
- defines proposed actions
- establishes expectations or success criteria
- states who is responsible
- sets a time scale
- identifies resource needs
- is concise; it needs to fit with all the others from different subjects.

A SCHEME OF WORK

- describes how the policy is delivered in practice
- offers guidance to teachers
- puts content into order
- explains what materials will be used
- explains how resources are organised
- defines which techniques will be used for what purposes with which children
- defines the approaches for children with special needs
- is detailed or it tells people where to turn to for advice

A BOOKLET FOR PARENTS

- helps the parents to see how they can support their children's development in English
- is written in friendly, jargon-free language
- gives examples of how learning usually takes place
- shows parents where there can sometimes be problems

STAFF GUIDELINES

- provide ideas and starting points
- offer examples of planning
- give sample lessons
- list resources
- contain examples of children's work
- offer plans for displays
- suggest useful educational visits
- contain book lists for teachers
- keep changing

A POLICY STATEMENT

- states some principles for the teaching of English in the school
- states the agreed aim
- states what the school expects the learners of English to be like as they leave the school
- states how English should be taught
- describes the assessment and record keeping procedures
- will be based on the Programmes of Study for National Curriculum English
- describes how adults will be involved
- is short

ASSESSMENT AND RECORDING PORTFOLIO

- guides school understanding on assessment and recording
- contains examplars at each level
- offers advice on recording methods
- suggest 'what then' is relevant

THIS IS FOR ONE SUBJECT. REMEMBER . . . . . .
YOU HAVE TO READ ANOTHER NINE OF THESE. KEEP IT BRIEF.

FIG 10.1
Documentation for a subject

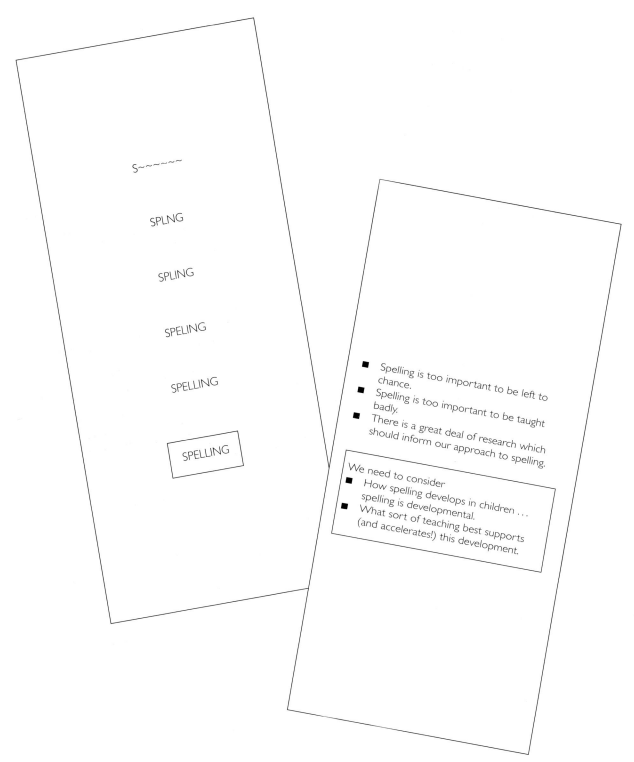

S~~~~~~

SPLNG

SPLING

SPELING

SPELLING

SPELLING

- Spelling is too important to be left to chance.
- Spelling is too important to be taught badly.
- There is a great deal of research which should inform our approach to spelling.

We need to consider
- How spelling develops in children . . . spelling is developmental.
- What sort of teaching best supports (and accelerates!) this development.

FIG 10.2
An example of an effective booklet for staff guidelines

Spelling Development

An awareness of how children develop their spelling is very important. It means we can appreciate what they are trying to do when they make spelling errors. Not all errors are the same!

1 Pre-Phonological Spelling — mark making, imitating adults (?????), using shapes (some of which resemble letters of the alphabet).

2 Phonological Spelling — the child realises that the letters of the alphabet stand for sounds (the 'alphabetic' principle).

- Uses the initial letter to stand for the word — mdisgtshps (my dad is going to the shops)
- Only writes the consonants (vowels are more difficult to hear in words) — shps (shops), lm (lamb), pncks (pancakes),
- Invents spelling based on the sounds in the word — siesajs (sausages), fiduld (fiddled).

Phonological spelling is a tremendous breakthrough for a young child. However if spelling remains 'sound based' it will not develop into conventional spelling.

3 Visual Spelling — this is the aim. Spelling is mainly about visual awareness. Good spellers develop a visual memory for how words look.

- We see this first in spellings such as pncks (pancakes). Why has the child used k? The child has noticed (seen) that pancakes contain k. Another example: appls — Why the double p?
- A child increasingly uses common letter strings: ough, ight, tion. In English it is always 'ough' (never uogh, ouhg…) although the sound may vary (though, through, thorough, enough …). Recognition of these common orthographic clusters is the key to good spelling.

4 Conventional Spelling — based on a visual memory of how words look (when faced with needing to use a word we cannot spell, how many of us write it two or three ways and choose the one which looks correct?)

[Because visual letter clusters are the key to spelling, handwriting is of great importance. Joined handwriting rather than printing is the aim once a child can form the letters correctly. So, 'ing' becomes a 'package' rather than three separate letters. For more details see Cripps and Cox, Joining the ABC, LDA, 1989]

FIG 10.2
(cont'd)

Spelling In The Classroom

Successful teaching of spelling is based around four basic principles.

1   When children are doing their own writing they have a go at every word.

- They gain confidence as writers.
- They use the 'best' words rather than playing safe (and only using words they can spell).
- The struggle with a word is vital for their learning.
- Spelling does not get in the way of composing — 'first get what is in your head onto paper'.
- They do not waste time in spelling queues and congas.

This can be very difficult to establish with children lacking in confidence, but it must be done. A whole school approach is vital.

In order to develop such confidence, it may be worth considering:

- In the early stages, encouraging children to focus on the opening sound and put a 'magic line' for the rest of the word:

     j____ (jump),   d__ (dog).

  Then trying both the opening and final sounds:

     j____p,   d__g.

  Finally we can consider the middle of the sandwich.

- This can lead to children underlining words they are not sure about: as they are writing.

     amrecan (American),
     speling (spelling).

2   Checking spelling takes place *after* the writing. This can be done:

- By the child.
- By children in pairs, helping each other.
- With the teacher — the key is to generalise from the error. For example the error is 'litel' — show the child 'little', show a couple of other 'le' words (cattle, topple), give the child a challenge to find six or more. In this way eight or nine words are learnt from one error (the child uses LOOK — COVER — WRITE — CHECK to learn the words).

[Dictionaries, word banks etc. are important, but after the writing]

3   Lessons which focus on spelling should be based on:

- A fascination with and enthusiasm for language (on the part of the teacher!)
- Class/group/individual challenges.
  'How many words can we find which end in 'ing'/begin with ch/have five syllables …'
  'Turn them into a piece of writing/a poem'.
  'Enjoy playing with the words, their patterns and their sounds'.

[Spelling challenges are positive, weekly spelling tests are negative. Assessment is best carried out with spelling dictations]

The most successful teachers of spelling

- Give children the *confidence* to have a go.
- View learning errors as positive features of a child's work.
- Share their own *fascination* for words with children.
- Use their *knowledge* of spelling development to analyse a child's errors.
- Encourage children to take responsibility for their own work and to check each other's spelling.
- Try to ensure that children view spelling as something positive and that SPEL does not become a four letter word (Richard Gentry, *Spel Is A Four Letter Word*, Scholastic, 1987).

A worthwhile resource:
Spelling In Context by Margaret Peters and Brigid Smith, NFER — Nelson, 1993 — lots of advice for teachers in terms of both classroom strategies and spelling assessment. Contains spelling dictations.

University College of St Martin, Rydal Road, Ambleside
LA22 9BB
Tel: (015394) 30250 Fax: (015394) 30289 E.mail Address:
INSET@UCSM.ac.uk

FIG 10.2
(*cont'd*)

Part four Monitoring for quality

Chapter 11

Monitoring classroom practice

Every now and again a new word comes into the language of teaching. In the last few years, monitoring has become one of those words. If you want to run your subject well or run your school well, you have to monitor. Lots of people worry about whether they're doing monitoring properly; lots of people worry about what it means. If we can work out what it means, we have a chance of doing it properly.

If we want to monitor something, we simply have to look at it, but we have to look with a purpose. In everyday life, in life outside education, we have monitors to keep an eye on things. Hotels often have closed circuit television cameras monitoring various entries to their property. Town centres nowadays have moved towards using closed circuit monitoring to keep an eye on public areas at all times. In hospitals, we have become used to patients being attached to monitors which give an instant readout of the state of health of various parts of the body. At airports, people readily agree to having their luggage monitored to check for items that should not be transported. All of these are examples of monitoring; keeping an eye on things. Within education, if we are to monitor successfully, we simply have to keep an eye on things; we have to be professionally nosy. Simply keeping an eye is not enough. If the hotel porter doesn't look at the monitors, then the body around the back does not get noticed. If the town centre cameras simply record what happens, but nobody looks at the monitor, then trouble spots don't get dealt with. In hospital, the patient doesn't receive the treatment necessary unless somebody keeps a check on the monitor. In the airport, looking at the luggage is one thing, noticing is another. And so it is in schools. Those responsible need to keep an eye and they need to check and they need to wonder whether what they are seeing is as it should be.

The coordinator of English, therefore, needs to keep a constant eye on what is happening and wonder whether the scheme of work and the guidelines offered to teachers are being put in place and whether children are achieving the sorts of expectations that we have of them. The trouble is that some people consider the motioning activity to be very threatening. For some, there are visions of playing at being OFSTED inspectors, moving from classroom to classroom with clipboard in place, filling out pro-formas, producing paragraphs, and casting judgment on all concerned. The OFSTED inspection is one form of monitoring, but it is only one form, and well-used in a school, its value can be immense, but there is no need to wait for four years at a time to monitor the work of the school. Monitoring should happen at all times, so that everybody, the coordinator or staff and senior management, are aware of what the issues are to do with the subject in the school. Monitoring means standing back, having a look, and asking questions. Those questions do not have to be too profound, too difficult, or too clever. We can ask simple questions that help us to be professionally nosy.

How well are they working?

To be in classroom and watch what is happening gives us the chance to ask how well the children are working. We can consider various things, for instance, we can consider various aspects of their English work.

■ **The product**
What are the children producing? We could look at the displays or their books and work out whether the children are producing the right amount of work, the right quality of work, whether they are having the chance to produce

writing which is across the range, including note-making, letter, diaries and factual writing.

■ **Children's ideas**

We could look at whether children are being allowed to express and use their own ideas. In speaking and listening to children, do they have a chance to dictate the agenda? In their reading, are children encouraged to think about how the story worked and how it could have ended? In writing, do children get to use their own ideas to do with content or presentation of their work?

■ **Speed**

How fast do they work? It is worth asking children when they start a piece of work when they expect to finish it? In some classes, children can do a considerable amount of writing in half an hour, whereas next door children can do half as much in twice the time.

■ **How hard are they working?**

To be in the classroom gives the opportunity to see the extent to which children are working hard. Do children have a work ethic?

■ **Effort**

How much effort do children appear to be putting in? When they come to a word they cannot write, do they simply stop and walk over to the teacher and ask for a spelling, or if children are reading, do they seem to be really engrossed in the book? This doesn't mean that children have to be working at the very limit of their ability, but it does mean that they have to be reading with rigour and making an effort to make sense of and enjoy the book. We have to work at enjoyment, it is not something that just happens. When children are taking part in speaking and listening activities, are they really engaged or do they just let the discussion go along?

■ **Purpose**

Children who are working hard usually understand the purpose of what they are doing. Simple questions like 'What are you doing and why?' draw out the extent to which children really understand the context of their English work. If they think they are simply working to please the teacher, are they fulfilling the expectations in staff guidelines? How hard are they working?

- **Presentation**

  How much effort are children making in presenting their work? This doesn't just apply to writing, although children who understand the different requirements of presentation at different stages of the writing process are meeting the needs of the National Curriculum. How much effort are children making in presenting their thoughts when talking to others? How much effort do they seem to be making when using a dictionary or looking up facts in a library book?

What qualities are seen in children?

The work in English is supposed to be contributing through the whole curriculum to the growth and development of every child. Therefore, during English sessions, we should see children being helped to develop the qualities that schools see as important.

- **Responsibility**

  Can we see, during English sessions, children having the chance to take responsibility? Do they 'have a go' at spelling and punctuation, or do they follow the teacher around the room, waiting for the teacher to spell the word or for the teacher to insert punctuation marks where necessary? Are children able to take responsibility for re-drafting and proof-reading, or does the teacher take it away from them?

- **Decision making**

  Are children able to choose, select, and make decisions about aspects of their work in English? Do they get the opportunity to select a book that they want to read or are they given the book they are expected to read? Are children allowed to read books that are far too 'easy' for them occasionally, or do they always have to work at their maximum level of challenge? Are children allowed to make decisions about who they work with and when and what for, or does the teacher decide all the groups?

■ **Consideration**

To what extent are children able to show consideration for the work of others? Does the very best work get praised and appreciated by all the class? Are the children who struggle given opportunities to show their best at appropriate times? Do the better children in English sometimes get the opportunity to support the less–good children? Do older children get the chance to work with younger children and use the skills that they have developed through the school?

Who is doing what?

If we get the chance to look into classrooms, we can ask what sort of work is going on with which children.

■ **Levels of work**

Are children doing work which is at their level? Is assessment and recording being used to indicate how children should move on within their subjects? Do children simply move through the reading scheme at the prescribed rate or is there a race? Or do children see level as something more than degree of difficulty, that reading can be getting to a deeper level in a plot or a deeper level in discussion?

■ **Grouping of children**

Are children just batched according to their own level of ability and simply moving around in a huddle of able or less able or average children, or does the teacher sometimes offer children the chance to work with people at different levels?

■ **With the teacher**

Who does the teacher work with? It is so easy in the classroom for the teacher to be sucked into working with the children who struggle, giving them most of the time and, in turn, most of the attention, so that the children who struggle rarely need to struggle for themselves. At the other extreme, those who can get on with a passing nod of acceptance from the teacher.

What sort of work is seen?

Is the range of English work seen across the subjects? Do we see English really influencing the whole curriculum? Do we see English being taught for its own sake?

- **All subjects**
  If we look in history, are we seeing children getting the chance to do note-taking; in geography, do we see the opportunity for quality speaking and listening; in design technology, are children using the opportunity to develop their understanding of recording and brainstorming; in physical education, do children get the chance to use speaking and listening as part of the lesson; in mathematics, are pupils encouraged to read and understand instructions, so that they can find their way through the scheme?

- **Skills and technicalities**
  How often do we see children taught the technicalities of punctuation and spelling? Are there opportunities to practise the skills they have learned without the practise becoming drudgery? Do the children develop skills such as dictionary work and reference work, so that they can apply them in context within other subjects?

- **Approaches**
  Do we see children approaching the subject from various angles and in different ways so that they are able to appreciate and understand the purpose and use of English in the subjects of the curriculum?

What is the teacher doing?

The way the teacher spends their time will influence the quality of learning for children and the standards they reach. Time in the classroom can reveal not just the teaching style, but the effectiveness of teaching and learning generally across the school in terms of the scheme of work.

■ **Demanding**

Does the classroom feel demanding and urgent or are children simply meandering through the curriculum? Is ERIC really Everybody Reading In Class or is it sometimes Everybody Rolling In Corners?

■ **Supervising**

Is the teacher so busy that he/she has no time for teaching, but merely supervises the children as they queue up with their endless lists of questions and can't dos?

■ **Observing**

Does the teacher have time to observe what children are doing and time to gauge which children are making progress at what rate in what area? Assessment . . .

■ **Teaching**

Is the teacher having time to teach? Does the teacher make planned opportunities to demonstrate to children or to lead the children by question and answer through a new set of challenges? Does the teacher plan to teach, for instance, technicalities such as spelling and punctuation, or are these taught only as and when issues arise?

What is the room like?

Just being in the room gives an opportunity to think about the teaching and learning that is taking place. You don't have to be in many classrooms to realise that the range of atmospheres is very, very different and therefore, will have a different impact upon the learning of the children.

■ **Fuss**

Is the room fussy? Sometimes, fuss is a good thing. If everyone in the class is involved in producing a class newspaper by three o'clock in the afternoon and distributing it to other classes, then we can expect some fuss, but is it controlled fuss that is well-managed and well-organised and that can be stopped at a moment's notice, or is it that fuss that comes about when children are a little unfocused and a little distracted? The trouble with being a little of a lot of things is that a lot of littles make a lot.

■ **Tidiness**

Children learn best when they are organised and efficient and one aspect of efficiency comes through tidiness. Are central areas for children well-organised; do children know how to use the book area; do they know how to get paper and use it properly; do they keep their own materials well-stored, so that the work they are doing is easily retrievable and unlikely to become dog-eared?

■ **Does the room have an organised feel?**

Do children and teachers know what is happening and what is going to happen next and why? Is there a feeling that there are clear deadlines and people are working to meet them or is it more a feeling of 'take your time and don't worry too much about being late'?

■ **Display**

Cast an eye around the room and get a feeling from the walls as to where English stands in the importance for children's learning. In so many schools, there is much writing on the walls, but so little comment is made about it. Is children's work there for decoration or is it there to influence future work? Do children get a chance to 'take part' in display or is it there to merely look at? Yet worse, is it there to keep people happy when they enter the room so that they think some good work has happened? Are the children interested in the display; do they know what is there; do they find it worth while to spend time enjoying?

All of these obvious questions relate to the task of monitoring classroom practice. Monitoring, using these questions, can take place on a very informal basis. It can be haphazard, it can be as and when, it can be wherever we happen to be. A true professional asks themselves questions all the time. The English coordinator should be asking questions about English wherever they are in school, whatever they are doing, to try to form a series of snapshots about what is happening within the subject. It is informal, it is imprecise, but it is monitoring.

Chapter 12

Assessment as a part of teaching

The co-ordinator has a major part to play in three key areas when it comes to assessment:

1   Ensuring that staff are aware of the complexities of assessment as children develop their ability to speak, listen, read and write.

2   Monitoring the ways in which detailed profiles of children are developed in school, to which both parents and the children themselves contribute.

3   Developing an ethos in which assessments are discussed and used to inform planning as children move from year to year.

The complexities of assessment

Assessment is not the same as tests, and there is a lot more to assessment than just giving children tests, be they at the end of the week, the end of the year or the end of the key stage. Indeed viewed purely internally, with no reference to how children are 'performing' in similar schools elsewhere, tests tell us very little. Some teachers argue that tests simply confirm what they already knew e.g. their most able readers do better than their least able readers. The real test, however, is whether the most able readers are achieving as much as children in other schools. We are not arguing here for league tables but on the place of standardised tests within the wider assessment process. They contribute to an assessment jigsaw for each child made up of three large pieces: summative, formative and diagnostic.

Summative

Assessments take place at the end of a period of work with a view to summing up a child's achievements. At the end of, say, Y4, what can be said about a child's ability as a reader or a writer or a speaker or a listener? SATs are summative assessments and so is the end of year report. Indeed the problem with SATs is that they can be seen as the only assessment worth worrying about, especially if the results are made public in the form of league tables. When the first such tables were published in the spring of 1997, one national newspaper wrote about the schools with 'the brightest pupils'.

In terms of test results of different kinds, schools build up sets of figures (scores, grades, reading ages, spelling ages, levels . . .) and in Chapter 13, 'Interpreting Data', we argue that these are most useful for asking questions about the school rather than individual children. We are right to be cautious and critical about what a particular test 'measures' (try writing down all of the processes involved in 'reading' and then look for a test which 'measures' all of them!) but we can discuss whether it might be telling us something important about the school. If only 5 per cent of Y6 gain Level 4 on the SAT, however critical we might be about the test, we may well want to investigate what is going on!

Formative assessment

Relates directly to the ways we teach English. It means being good at what is known as 'kid watching' in the USA, monitoring a child's progress as they develop their ability to listen, speak, read and write. Through such assessment, which goes on constantly in the classroom, we build up a picture of a child's strengths and weaknesses. Formative assessment is not, then, a separate aspect of teaching but a dynamic part of how we plan, execute and monitor what is happening in the classroom. As coordinator there are two major challenges:

■ Does the English curriculum with which the children are engaging enable proper formative assessment to be carried out? In this sense it should relate directly to the chapters in this book about English teaching. Are children reading a 'range' of texts? Are they writing different types of text for different purposes? Are they speaking and listening for different purposes in pairs, small groups, large groups and the class? We have argued that knowledge of what is meant by 'best practice' in English teaching is the foundation of the job of being an English coordinator. Enabling colleagues to develop the same knowledge is a major challenge and one which will impact directly on the quality of assessment going on in each classroom.

■ Is the ethos in classrooms such that children really will be showing us what they can do? So much of English is about confidence and risk taking that we must beware of assuming that what we get in the context of a classroom is a true reflection of a child's strengths and interests:

In terms of **oracy**, is the 'quiet' child who never volunteers more than the shortest possible utterance (and then only when asked directly) 'weak' as a speaker? Or does this reluctance stem from the classroom situation as much as the child? Does it actually reflect the way in which speaking is viewed in this class? Or the dominant style of questioning being employed by the teacher? Simple shifts in teaching practice can often produce dramatic changes in how we assess a child. For example, when working with the whole class we have a choice of addressing our questions to the children either as individuals, or sets of pairs or sets of small groups. If the first, we are unlikely to get every child volunteering to answer and certainly will not be able to have each child actually contributing. If the second, all children will speak to each other (this works from Reception to Y6) and can agree an answer. If the third, most children will speak — indeed we can engineer it so that each child does so. We might 'target' particular children on different occasions, take note of how they respond to the different situations and add this information to our developing assessments of them. As a result we might plan to incorporate more of a particular questioning strategy into our teaching.

Of course a child might still be a very different speaker (and listener) outside the classroom, in the playground or at home. Teachers often comment about the surprising changes in children when they are taken away on school trips. How far does this 'count' for assessment, or is it only based on what goes on in the confines of the classroom? Given such considerations it is arguable that we are not really able to assess 'oracy'. Each of us can imagine situations in which we would not be forthcoming as speakers, perhaps have recently attended meetings and said very little. This is why we must ensure our assessments take account of different situations involving different people and that even so we view them with a full realisation of the complexities involved.

It is salutory to consider that to say a child has or has not made progress in **reading** is only really to say that the child has or has not made progress on a particular reading programme. A different rate of progress may well have been made on a different programme. In Chapter 5 we examined the idea of 'literary competence' which describes a reader's growing awareness of the ways in which different texts work. Such competence, to be able to deal with different types of text for different purposes, is a key element in reading assessment at Key Stage 2. Whether it is ongoing, teacher, formative assessment or a standardised test we must be aware of the text being read.

However, the same concerns about the classroom as the only context for assessment apply to reading. We have met many children who have contrasting things to say about the reading they do at home and that which occupies them at school. This may simply be in terms of one type of reading, such as the Y6 child who had recently read Tolkein's *Lord Of The Rings* and *The Silmarillion* at home while having to read from the reading scheme at school! Sometimes it means we can be unaware of complex, home reading matter, for example computer handbooks, which are not represented in the classroom.

Just as speaking in formal situations is bound up with confidence, so the same is true of **writing**. Is the ethos in the classroom one which encourages children to 'have a go' and use the best words even though they might not know how to spell them? Can they indicate these to the teacher in the ways we discussed earlier knowing that these 'learning errors' will be viewed positively and used as the basis for teaching points? The alternative in which children 'play safe' and only use the words they are sure about ('nice' instead of 'beautiful') will result in dubious assessment of their writing ability.

Ongoing, formative assessment is complex. If it is to contribute meaningfully to the developing profile of a child's ability in English it is important that all teachers are aware of this.

Diagnostic assessment

Involves looking closely at what a child knows and can do. It takes time and therefore needs to be planned. It is worthwhile focusing staff meetings on such assessment both in terms of what exactly is being assessed and how such assessment might be managed in the busy classroom. In terms of **speaking and listening** it could mean targeting a particular group of children for a week, taking note of how they 'perform' in terms of the areas outlined in Chapter 6 For **reading** there will be decisions about whether a miscue analysis or running record would be useful, generally for the younger children or those about whom we are concerned. For the majority we might target particular children each week to observe in paired or guided reading situations. Diagnostic assessment of a child's **writing** may not be feasible for every piece in a large class, however, we can target six different children each time. We will respond to all the children and they will be unaware that we have been engaging in diagnostic assessment on only six. However we manage such assessment, in writing there is also the danger that we will let our assessment be dominated by the secretarial skills of spelling, punctuation and handwriting. While these are vitally important we must always be aware of the need to assess progress in other areas, for example at the text level, the quality of the content itself and the ways in which a child has organised the piece — how it opens, how it develops and how it ends. At the sentence level we might look at the proficiency with which a child can use the language of the genre or, perhaps, note the appearance of complex sentences or the passive tense. A meeting with KS2 staff in which examples of writing from children in the school are diagnostically assessed is well worth considering. This will ensure that pieces of writing kept as evidence of progress really do reflect the above and are useful to teachers who receive them as the child moves up the school.

Monitoring profiles

Summative, formative and diagnostic assessments all contribute to a developing profile of individual children. Above we have stressed the need to ensure that the curriculum and ethos in a classroom enable children to demonstrate their skills and knowledge. We have also raised the problem of the classroom being the only context for assessment. It follows that, in addition to teachers, other people should contribute to assessment profiles if they are to provide a full picture of a child's progress.

Firstly, children themselves should be contributing and this can happen in a number of ways. Perhaps the two most important are:

1   Children keeping their own records of what they have been doing. In Chapter 5 we discussed a Reading Diet sheet which draws attention to the need for a child to engage in a range of reading of different genres. A similar Writing Diet record makes a similar point (for a teacher as much as for a child!). It would be interesting to consider a Speaking and Listening record of the different ways in which a child

worked (as an individual, in a pair, in a small group, in a large group, as part of the 'whole class').

Added to these records can be comments by the child about what they have been reading, what they felt were the strengths and weaknesses of their own writing and how they felt about working in different situations. Other children can also contribute, as this example of children 'criticising' their own and each other's topics indicates (see Figure 12.1).

FIG 12.1
Topic evaluation sheets

Topic evaluation

Topic Exploration and Encounters

Date Tuesday 10th November

Author Elizabeth Evans

Critic Katy Beasley

Five things I am impressed by;

1 The front cover because its very neat.

2 The diary because its very interesting.

3 The Aztec drawing because it looks like the picture in the book.

4 The Aztec food because it looks real.

5 The bearings because its lifelike.

Five things which could be improved;

1 The neatness because it looks a bit messy.

2 The picture of Columbus because it has too many skech mark.

3 The codex pocket because its wringkled.

4 The co-ordinate pairs because I did not know what the cracker was at first.

5 The writing because its too fancy on the Aztec food.

Comment

I think on the whole Elizabeths folder is very good.

FIG 12.1
(cont'd)

Topic evaluation

Topic <u>Exploration and Encounters</u>

Date <u>10th November 1992</u>

Author <u>Elizabeth Evans</u>

Critic <u>Elizabeth Evans</u>

<u>Five things I am impressed by;</u>

1 <u>On my Columbus writing my picture of the Santa maria was good because I did good shading.</u>

2 <u>My picture of a banana is good on my Aztec food because it was detailed.</u>

3 <u>I think my Sun God writing was good because I put the writing in a good order.</u>

4 <u>I like my Aztec drawing because I put lots of diferent colours on it.</u>

5 <u>I think my pictures on my bearings are good because they are quite imaganative.</u>

<u>Five things which could be improved;</u>

1 <u>Sometimes my writing gets a bit scruffy.</u>

2 <u>On my front piece the parrot has got a bit of a small head and it spoils it a bit.</u>

3 <u>Sometimes when I rub out it leaves a mark.</u>

4 <u>I think I could have done the picture of Columbus better because his face dosn't look right and he's frowning.</u>

5 <u>I could have done the pocket for my diary better because its a bit wrinkled.</u>

<u>Coments</u>

I think my folder has turned out quite well because I understood what I had to do and I just did it as quickly well and clearly writen as I could without spelling anything. Sometimes I had a mistake but I've corrected it as well as I could.

2   In depth interviews with a teacher. These can take place half termly, so that a teacher's aim is to 'interview' each child each term. The agenda should cover how the child feels about the different areas of English and what they consider to be their strengths and weaknesses as well as what they have been reading and writing at home as well as at school.

Secondly, parents can provide information which might not be gathered from any other source. Traditionally such discussions were one way only, with the school passing to the parent information about their child. Increasingly the benefits have been recognised of the school finding out what sorts of reading, writing and speaking experiences go on at home. Does the child read alone or with other children or particular adults? How is homework tackled? How do the parents help? In addition parents know their perceptions and concerns are taken seriously and they are able to raise particular issues. Children know that their parents are involved in their school lives.

Using assessment

The gathering of information made up of the different aspects described above can provide a rich picture of a child's progress in English. As we argue throughout this book, so much depends on the knowledge of the teacher so that they are able to recognise what we mean by strengths and weaknesses and how we recognise progress. Ensuring that assessment is actually discussed and used in school is vital if it is not to be viewed as a 'bolt on' to teaching. We have already mentioned useful meetings at which writing is analysed, an exercise which certainly helps all of us develop our awareness of assessment. Other aspects can be a focus for similar meetings. Teachers can discuss what they learnt from each observing six children as speakers and listeners over the course of a week. The Reading Diet or Writing Diet sheets can be brought to a meeting. A running record of a particular child's reading can be the focus. Such meetings will not only ensure that assessment is seen as more than just the SAT results or the end of the week spelling test, but are a valuable way for the coordinator to raise awareness and increase teacher knowledge of the English curriculum.

Chapter 13   Interpreting data and setting targets

One way of looking closely at the effectiveness of teaching in English is to use available data to shed light. Since the onset of the move towards comparing school performance there has been a growing supply of statistical information. There are many arguments about the reliability and validity of the data and the way it is gathered and used. Within the school, whatever the views on the data, it cannot be ignored as a source of information and an opportunity to review teaching and learning in English. The coordinator needs to able to use this source of information to find out whether the school is achieving the highest standards for its children. Put simply, we need to be able to answer the question, **'How well are we doing?'**

What data is available?

SATs

Year 6 is tested on an annual basis. The information can be used in each individual year and on a year on year basis to give a picture, though very limited, of the attainment of children in a limited range of the English curriculum.

At Year 2, just before they enter Key Stage 2, children are tested annually. This gives a starting and end point measure, even on this limited criteria, for the four year period. As the tests evolve and become more standardised, the growing amount of data will provide valuable evidence of progress.

Along with the SATs come Teacher Assessments and these provide further data to consider.

League tables

The league tables might be resented, welcomed or ignored, possibly depending where the school finds itself in the list. Whatever the merits or faults, the system is here and rather than simply teaching to the test to rise up the table as others drop down, it might be possible to tease out whether the tables say anything about the performance of the school, especially when compared with 'like schools'. Many LEAs have statistics departments which can provide analysis for a school helping it to compare with schools of similar catchment by free meals, social conditions, statements for special educational need, ethnicity, and so on. These departments can break down information within the school to show performance of girls, boys, ethnic groups, or children with English as an additional language. This information is useful within school in allowing comparison but also in terms of highlighting issues to address. So, regardless of the political battles over league tables, there is information to be gained.

PICSI

No, not loveable little characters at the end of the garden: Pre-Inspection Context and School Indicator (PICSI) Report, data that is produced by OFSTED before the school inspection . . . what was that about loveable little characters? The inspection team is provided with a batch of statistics and a copy is given to the school. Many schools find this a useful source of information.

PANDAs

No, not a loveable little creature with doleful eyes: Performance and Assessment documents are superseding PICSIs. Yes, PICSI are taken over by PANDAs! What is education coming to? We thought it was getting intense and market driven on an industrial model when the truth is that little toys are really in charge!

Each school will have a PANDA document which offers the school a chance to compare itself statistically with all others, with others of its own socio-economic grouping and with others of similar size. The PANDA provides information similar to the PICSI but adds a comparison of information and grading from school inspections. This means that a school can look at its own inspection report and compare the comments, say, for the management of English, with schools generally.

Standardised tests

Although the national system of testing is becoming established, many schools use standardised tests to give a measure of progress for individual children, to highlight a range of special needs, to give a yardstick for performance year on year, or to keep an eye on progress of year groups of children if they are split between classes.

Some LEAs provide tests for pupils at particular ages to identify the need for provision of special needs support. Even though the purpose of such tests is an LEA 'sweep' the information is useful to an individual school in giving the same opportunities as its own school-based test.

What can data tell us?

If we have information, then we need to analyse it. We can look at the data and see whether it is telling us anything. We need to consider the difference between

- the school and the results for the rest of the country;
- the school and the results for the rest of the LEA;
- the results for different subjects and English;
- the teacher assessments and the SATs;
- the performance of boys and girls;
- the results for different Attainment Targets;
- the results for different classes;
- this year and previous years;
- this year and the previous best.

Given the sort of picture that this information and analysis can paint, we should not only be able to answer the question, 'How well are we doing?' but we should be able to articulate an argument to answer the question, **'How well should we be doing?'**

Looking at some examples

SATs and Teacher Assessment

We can start with how well we did. We should be achieving the average number of Level 4s. If we did we can be satisfied, or can we? We cannot just leave it at that; we need to look underneath the surface at the questions above. Some schools spend time analysing the individual answers to the SAT questions, finding out what the children could and could not do and modifying planning for the future accordingly. This can be useful in looking for trends but it can be a terrible waste of time and produce knee jerk reactions which are unnecessary and have little impact year on year. There is no doubt though that analysis might highlight that the school currently places too little emphasis upon punctuation or puts lots of effort into reading without giving children opportunity to develop inference through effective discussion of texts.

Looking at the results in context can be useful. Figure 13.1 is from a PICSI Report and shows the attainment of pupils in one school at the end of Key Stage 2.

On the face of it the children are achieving reasonably well. The PICSI, though gives opportunity to compare with the national scene by offering further information and analysis (see Figure 13.2).

While the school is well above the average at Level 4, it is around the average at Level 5. This could mean that the school is doing well to push its children up to the average or failing to stretch the more able into the Level 5 area. The PICSI also compares Teacher Assessments with the national averages and offers information (see Figure 13.3).

FIG 13.1
Chart showing attainment at end of
Key Stage 2

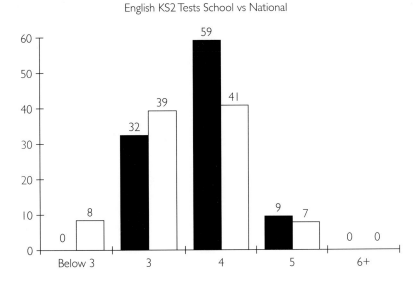

English KS2 Tests School vs National

FIG 13.2
Results based on the KS2 tests

On the basis of the tests:

The percentage of pupils reaching Level 4 or above — 68 per cent — was well above the national average.

The percentage of pupils reaching Level 5 or above — 9 per cent — was not significantly different from the national average.

FIG 13.3
Results on basis of the teacher assessments

On the basis of the teacher assessments:

The percentage of pupils reaching Level 4 or above — 79 per cent — was well above the national average.

The percentage of pupils reaching Level 5 or above — 28 per cent — was well above the national average.

In both Level 4 and Level 5 the Teacher Assessments are well above the national average. The reason could be that the teachers over-estimate the pupils, or the pupils under-perform on the tests, or the teachers are not providing well for the more able. Whatever the reason for the discrepancy, the thinking about reasons might shed light upon issues of classroom practice which need to be addressed.

Standardised tests

The tests may be suspect but they are usually quick to administer and provide that chance to notice the issues. An example is offered below of the year on year scores of Year 6 pupils using The London Reading Test in Figures 13.4a and 13.4b.

FIG 13.4a
Year 6 Standardised reading results: Percentage achieving a score less than 85

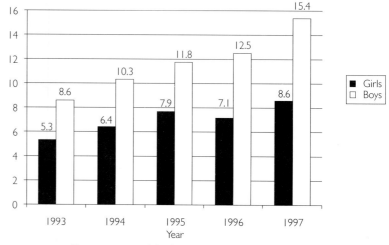

The percentage population in this range of normal distribution is 16%

FIG 13.4b
Year 6 Standardised reading results: Percentage achieving a score of 115 and over

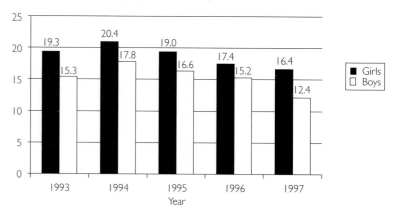

The percentage population in this range of normal distribution is 16%

We might debate the testing issues, such as whether the vocabulary is within the context of the children, but there are trends to spot and questions to ask. For this group of schools the number of struggling readers is rising year on year. For this group of schools the proportion of boys doing poorly at reading is rising. The schools may have been in changing social circumstances for these years, there may be more problems, there may be other influences on the children, but there is a need to do something quickly to help the strugglers in reading or so much of their secondary curriculum is unavailable to them. There are needs for these children as they enter Key Stage 3 that are likely to continue through that Key Stage. As teachers in each school review their efforts in the teaching of reading there is a further need to consider what might be done to halt the trend of boys falling into the struggling zone. Is it resources, methods, approaches, time or lack of parental support? The data offers the issue; the schools need to react.

Individual schools need to study their own standardised test information. It is plain from Figures 13.5a and 13.5b that the schools concerned perform differently and achieve different results in terms of reading levels. To stop at whether we are doing well or badly is to miss a cue.

If this is the picture of reading in each school, should the provision not be different to cater for the children in each school? One of these schools should be offering demanding texts, extending and stretching the reader. Another should be providing different opportunities, different texts, different discussions about books and different uses of books in other curriculum areas. They all need to be thinking about how children are presented with tasks in other subjects and how reading is offered to children to allow them to succeed.

FIG 13.5a
Chart illustrating test results

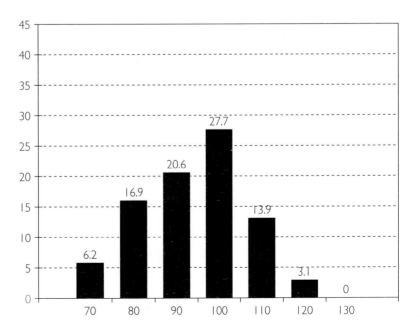

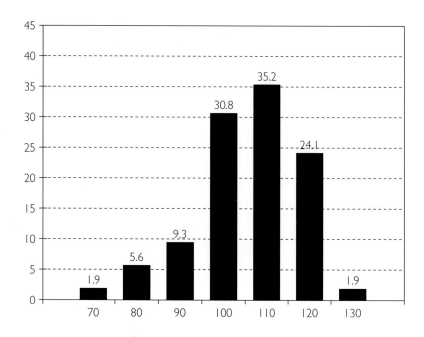

FIG 13.5b
Chart illustrating test results

What could be the issues?

We need to look at the data and consider the issues; ask what it is that we would wish to question further. What could be the factors?

- parental outlook/culture
- purposeful curriculum
- relationships
- teacher enthusiasm
- gender culture
- interest and motivation

- assessment
- teacher knowledge
- ethnic culture
- classroom management
- resources
- accommodation

Considering the issues

It is all about asking questions, saying what does this data tell us? The questions do not have to be complicated or difficult, just provoke honest answers.
- Are policies in place?
- Are children getting a good experience?
- Is anything being neglected?

- Are there any trends or blips?
- What are the reasons?
- Is the tone changing in English?
- Is our work efficient?

Do figures speak for themselves?

We have to be so careful with figures. They can conceal as much as they show, but they can give pointers and clues that, linked to our knowledge of the background of the school, can tell us how well we are doing. If we know how well we are doing we can decide whether it is well enough. The trouble with teachers is that they are always prepared to put their efforts down and want better than they are achieving. Nowadays though, the pressure is on. The world at large wants more.

Most teachers want children to achieve more and believe their schools are capable of improvement but it is now a legal requirement for a school to set targets for its level of attainment on an annual basis. These targets have to be quantifiable which means that we have to take account of data in order to use it effectively.

Setting targets

What more can we aim to achieve?

The challenge of the annual targets is significant. If we set targets that are too high we aim to fail, too low and we become complacent. Set new targets but fail to change practice and there will be little hope of raising standards. The issues referred to above need to be addressed and practice needs to be modified, but that does not mean we need to teach to the test. Most schools want to look at attainment and standards alongside the general achievement of children. They want to see learning and the aims of education in a wider dimension that the three 'R's. If children get the sorts of experiences described in this book then standards will rise. If the expectations of the Programmes of Study are to be met then teaching to the test will not succeed and at the next inspection there will be criticisms of schools rising up the tables with rising results but failing to provide the range required.

The whole school is involved in setting targets, the senior management, the staff and the governors. The coordinator can offer advice and justification about the level to be set but it is for the whole school to agree on the level. The LEA has a responsibility to set targets for all the schools within its control and then to analyse the targets of each school to check that the average of the targets will ensure that the LEA as a whole achieves the level expected.

A good rule for targets, often talked about in management books, is that they should be **SMART; simple, measurable, attainable, realistic and time specific**. In the case of standards in English in a school this can be made to work.

Think about the time limits

A good target will state that, for instance, 'the school will raise the proportion of pupils achieving Level 4 in reading by . . . % within . . . years'. The time span is essential. If the target is annual the implication is that the teachers of Year 6 are the ones responsible for action. Over a few years it is everyone's responsibility and a staggered target means that practice has to develop from Year 2 onwards in order to achieve the desired effect. So an annual target is fine as long as it fits into a long-term picture. In setting the targets, start with the long-term picture, say five years, and then put in the staging points along the way, with a gradually rising expectation to reach the goal.

Decide on sensible targets

If everyone aims for the moon will there be enough fuel to get there? If science and maths and English are all going on all cylinders will the engine cope? There needs to be negotiation between subjects, maybe priorities year on year. It is a good idea to consider setting targets at two levels; realistic and ambitious. They can be reviewed annually.

Set some targets that are not SATs driven

'80 per cent of Year 5 children will be able to lead a group discussion' or '95 per cent of Year 4 children will choose to take home a poetry book by the end of the year'. Targets like this, made known to parents, governors and children, where appropriate, help to show that improvement is not just about cramming for the test but has a much wider basis in the general education of the child.

Celebrate achieving the targets

The teaching profession is notorious for achieving things and not telling anyone; we just move on to the next problem. Plan to review targets, announce the results, address problems and celebrate successes. Announce successes to the whole school community, including the outside community.

Set targets and say how

If we intend to raise standards through gradual improvement then we have to do something to make it better. We can try to raise reading standards by reading 'harder' but we might need to do something else. It is hard to lose weight just by standing on scales; we need to modify the diet and take planned exercise. So how will we modify the diet and plan new exercise to achieve the targets in English? When athletes want to improve performance they plan programmes to achieve their goals, they develop new regimes. In teaching, we need to change programmes, routines and regimes to enhance performance and we can do this by confronting the issues and by setting expectations in the wider sense about good practice in teaching. To achieve targets we do not just do more of it; we do it better. By setting expectations about the way in which targets will be addressed, we are making explicit statements to answer the question, **'What must we do to make it happen?'**

This means setting 'sub-targets'

We need to set the targets that lay out the programme that helps us to achieve the overall targets. Saying we want children to read better involves a whole range of dimensions in reading practice in school. How will teachers modify their work to help children to read better? The issues discussed in the chapter on reading will point the way to changes of practice. Chapter 9, on producing a development plan, will highlight ways to structure the modification of teaching to ensure that targets are addressed.

Some sub-targets might be
- all children will take part in group reading for thirty minutes three times per week;
- a poem will be discussed at least once a week;
- children will be taught the skills necessary to use the reference library by the end of Year 2.

Expectations of this sort will raise the standards of reading in the school but bring with them some challenges in terms of **'making it happen'**; that is where the idea of the subject development plan comes in.

To complete the cycle it is necessary to check that the setting of targets actually had some effect. Were targets achieved? Are we keeping to schedule? Are people able to do what is expected of them or do they need further training to help us to hit the targets? If we are doing better than expected, are the targets right? This takes us back to the beginning, to reviewing the current position and knowing how well we are doing.

An example can be helpful to get going on something like target setting. What follows in Figure 13.6 is a breakdown of examples to show the sort of things that could be included.

Target Setting — examples — KS2 English		Lancashire County Council

Goal — To improve literacy in the school.

Headline target — To increase number of children attaining Level 4 at KS2 by 10%.

Action — Review past SATs papers and analyse areas of weakness.

Outcome/evidence

a) Children underattain in spelling of unconventional words e.g. 'echo', 'stadium'.

b) High-achieving children underattain in handwriting through underdeveloped personal fluent cursive style.

c) Lower-achieving children underattain in handwriting through use of irregular ascenders/descenders.

d) Boys underperform in writing through:

        (i) overuse of limited themes e.g. fantasy and science fiction

        (ii) failure to maintain a sense of audience

e) Girls with English as an additional language underperform in writing through:

        (i) use of limited vocabulary and metaphor

        (ii) difficulty in finding subject matter beyond the daily routine

f) Children underperform in reading by:

        (i) failing to analyse the authors' techniques in providing an effect on an audience

        (ii) being unable to cite evidence from the text for their opinion

        (iii) being unable to draw general conclusions about a situation or character

g) Boys underperform in reading by: (i) finding difficulty in engaging with 'un-macho' texts e.g. dismissing all female characters as 'silly'

(NB Not all — these are examples of what *could* be identified.)

ASSESSMENT OUTCOME	TARGET (for 1st year)	ACTION	SUCCESS CRITERIA
a)	15% improvement	Ensure teaching of spelling includes focus on word derivation throughout KS2. Children to understand roots and history of words. Link with history — Greeks and Romans.	Children show interest and can discuss origin of common words. Able to name words from common root.
b)	20% improvement	Ensure children with well-developed skills experience wide range of good models and be encouraged to experiment with personal style and to self-evaluate for speed, efficiency and appearance.	Able to express and explain preferences and try out styles while maintaining clear letter formation.
c)	30% improvement	Observe letter formation carefully; take children showing problems back to appropriate point (e.g. letters in air, sand etc.), use range of appropriate materials e.g. differently lined paper; set weekly goals for practice, agreed with child.	Clear signs of improvement which child is able to discuss and evaluate.

FIG 13.6
Examples of target setting

ASSESSMENT OUTCOME	TARGET (for 1st year)	ACTION	SUCCESS CRITERIA
d)	5% improvement	(i) Ensure appropriate range of reading materials/authors used in class and available for home reading. Be aware of and use recommendations of QCA's 'Boys and English' study, e.g. consider appropriate reading partners, use of male role models (visitors?) for both reading and writing e.g. local football club. Use wide range of stimuli for writing, ensuing range of directions.	Boys show more interest in range of subjects and willingness to respond to stimuli.
		(ii) Offer range of real audiences e.g. write story for Y2 class to their specifications, constantly checking back and being evaluated by Y2. Write to governors on school issue and ask sympathetic Governor questions to respond to appropriate texts. Ditto shopkeeper etc., with complaints. Constantly relate to real life. Read texts which highlight audience.	Greater awareness shown — clear attempt to adapt style to purpose.
e)	5% improvement	(i) Use bilingual support to examine descriptive language and metaphor in mother tongue poetry etc. Ensure sufficient English vocabulary is familiar. Role-model appropriate writing and examine range of texts. Play vocabulary games e.g. 'Call my Bluff' and 'Who am I'.	Greater confidence in range of description and willingness to try the uncommon.
		(ii) Ensure wide range of reading texts and other language experiences e.g. story-telling (teacher or tape or visitor). Find real or fictional role-models for females of varied ethnic background engaging in wider activities (e.g. Schools' TV drama). Choose appropriate 'response partner' to support and stimulate writing. Ensure range of stimuli is attractive.	Evidence of a wider approach and more confidence in imagining other roles.
f)	10% improvement	(i) (ii) (iii) Read a wide variety of texts with and to children, fiction and non-fiction and discuss responses. Maintain a 'reading journal' to note observations. Use range of strategies before, during and after reading e.g. 'First Steps' materials to support analysis and draw general inferences. Use further range of non-paper texts, e.g. video to develop inferential skills — stories or even soap operas. Analyse characters, predict future development to story line using evidence from past. Examine characters who show both 'good' and 'bad' qualities together.	Children able to refer to features of text e.g. headings, type face, layout and describe effort; ditto choice of vocabulary and sentence structure. Children able to describe and discuss complex character i.e., beyond 'nasty/nice'.
g)	10% improvement	See d) and (i) and f) and specific choice of texts, anonymous texts/characters (i.e., can they tell male from female authors and characters?)	Evidence of more open-minded approach.

FIG 13.6
(cont'd)

The area of target setting is a difficult one in terms of philosophy for many schools. Visions of graphs on walls and monthly out-turns do not always sit well in a profession that has tended to shun the output in favour of the input. It does seem important, though, to recognise that if we have information we may as well use it wisely to help the children achieve more. Most schools are able to say what they want children to be able to do as they leave them. If you can say what you want, you should be able to say whether you achieve it. Sometimes we might need to be able to offer more than gut feelings or hearsay. Data can have some value when used sensibly and in moderation.

Chapter 14

Preparing for inspection

Most teachers have now had the experience of being inspected. For some it was as bad as most of the stories said it would be. For most it was a professional experience which recognised the work that was being done and gave some pointers for future work. One of the problems has been that the horror stories become more dramatic in the telling and the myths and legends grow. There are bound to have been schools which have had bad experiences but the overwhelming picture is of schools finding the inspection process useful. It may have been stressful, hard work, deflecting from the agenda the school was working on, and a bit of a let-down afterwards, but it was professionally useful. As schools get re-visited, there will be more confidence, more awareness of the process, more initiative taken by the schools rather than 'having it done to them', and a better use of the chance to review the work of the school using an agreed agenda.

As the inspection approaches there are some things that the coordinator can do to prepare. The first thing is to be acquainted with what is on the inspectors' agenda.

What are OFSTED inspectors looking for?

The framework for inspection is available to all schools and explains what it is that inspectors make judgments upon when inspecting a school. For each subject there is the same range of enquiry and, of course, English is complex because of the relationship of each element to the rest of the curriculum. If we look at reading as an example, the inspectors have much to find out, then just mirror the process for other aspects.

The inspectors look at **Attainment and Progress** in the subject.

They need to observe:

- the range, accuracy and fluency of pupils' reading;
- pupils' ability to read;
- pupils' ability to understand and respond to literary and other texts;
- how consistent use of good literature and a variety of non-literary texts offer pupils a lifelong source of enjoyment and information;
- how pupils employ a range of strategies for reading, including phonic skills, word recognition and the use of picture and context clues.

The inspectors also observe **Attitudes, behaviour and personal development**

In reading they examine how well:

- pupils understand what they read;
- remember and enjoy what they read;
- independently choose books;
- choose books for information and quality;
- use public libraries and IT resources.

The inspectors examine **Teaching**.

They want to know

- the extent of sequenced planning;
- the way resources are used to improve reading ability;
- that occasions are offered to pupils to read; an additional
- whether consideration is given to learners of English as a second language;
- if the teaching helps children to be fascinated by reading;
- whether the teaching is different for children with different needs.

To find out about these things the inspectors will listen to children read. They will talk to them about their reading and their likes and dislikes. They will talk with children about their reading to see whether they understand it and whether they are able to respond to the literature and poetry as well as glean information from non-fiction texts. They will see whether they can use dictionaries and indexes and whether they can find books in the library.

The inspectors will report on the **Assessment, recording and reporting of reading**.

Key questions include:

- How is assessment carried out and does it provide a clear and accurate picture of attainment?
- Does the school use the information gained in reading tests or SATs?
- Do the outcomes of assessment influence the teaching of reading?
- How is pupil performance and progress recorded?
- What is the quality of reports to parents? Are reports helpful?

The role of the coordinator is considered under the heading of **Leadership and Management**.

The inspectors will ask

- Has the role been clearly defined?
- Does the coordinator have a real overview of provision, standards, and quality?
- Does the coordinator have opportunity to monitor the work of the school in reading?
- How does the coordinator keep staff up to date?
- How are priorities identified in development plans?
- How does the coordinator influence teachers' planning?
- Does the coordinator control a budget for reading? How is value for money assured?

The inspectors will look at **Staffing, Resources and Accommodation**.

There will be interest in

- the way INSET opportunities have been provided and used;
- how INSET needs have been identified for reading;
- the quality of support for children with special needs;
- how the classrooms promote reading;
- the quality of library provision in classrooms and centrally;
- the range and quality of resources to support different strategies;
- the age of books, the storage and the upkeep;
- the proportion of books per pupil.

Getting ready: before the inspection

Looking around the school

Well before the inspection the coordinator can start the process of looking at what is going on. It is part of the general

Checklist of work in English

Subject:	Range	Skills	Link with other subjects	Progression
Display				
Resources				
Children's work				

monitoring role but can be a useful exercise at given points in the school year. As a staff, part of an in-service school closure day can be spent with everyone visiting other classes to look critically at aspects of work. This is one way to get coherence, continuity and progression in the curriculum. A simple walk around the classes, in pairs, using a checklist as a note pad, will raise questions for discussion about the appearance of subjects (see above).

Display and resources may not be the key features but they are issues that surround the children all the time and they will speak to the children about what matters in the school.

- Is there any poetry on display?
- Are there examples of writing for different purposes?
- Are library books stored effectively?
- Do children have a range of reading material presented to them?
- Are different types of writing used in different subjects?
- What evidence is there of speaking and listening being valued?

- How is good spelling encouraged?
- Are expectations growing as children get older?
- Do children exhibit a growing range of skills and abilities as they get older?
- Is the computer fully used?
- Does handwriting appear as legible and fluent in all subjects?
- Do children produce information in charts, diagrams and graphs?

All of these questions will be within the conversations to be had about work in school. Working in this way the staff can be the 'in-school' inspectors, picking up impressions from the messages around the school.

Thinking your job through

The inspection team will wish to interview the coordinator for English. This is rarely a nasty experience and the evidence from inspection follow-up is that many teachers enjoy the chance to talk about their role with someone from outside the school. It is a good idea to prepare; not in the sense of being interviewed and practising the answers, but thinking through the issues so that afterwards there are not things that you forgot or wished you had said. Few inspectors would object if the coordinator turned up with notes so imagining a conversation is a good place to start. What follows is a prompt sheet with the sort of questions an inspector might ask (Figure 14.1). To the questions have been added some bullet point answers as memory joggers for the conversation.

The list of aspects and questions used by inspectors can provide a checklist for the coordinator in school. Not all the questions can be answered straight away, not all the answers will be positive but if the questions are used as a starting point they might lead towards a realistic review of practice in English.

FIG 14.1
Examples of inspection questions

The job — what do you do?
- Set school aims and objectives for English, with staff.
- Organise whole school themes and activities.
- Provide INSET, support and ideas for staff.
- Foster curriculum continuity, balance, match and consistency, progression and practice throughout school.

How much time do you get to coordinate the subject?
- Time is available when it's needed, by negotiation, if I need to observe or monitor sessions.
- Non-contact time during assembly or singing is used too.

What are the problems associated with coordinating this subject?
- Tackling areas of concern and feeling satisfied I have done all I can is sometimes frustrating.
- Monitoring and supporting effectively in such a big school is time consuming!

How do you organise resources and spending for your subject?
- Spending allowances are allocated to each subject coordinator. I tend to buy resources by replacing old stock continuously whilst also focusing on an area I have identified as a weakness. It may need better or new resources.

What are the strengths and weaknesses of the subject?
- Speaking and Listening and Reading are strengths. Spelling and Storywriting are improving although Spelling is still not strong. Handwriting is a weakness.

How do you know?
- A recent LEA report confirmed what I had discovered through SAT analysis.
- Then I have a termly focus based on that analysis. During that term, I collect samples of work, provide INSET for staff and set whole school assessment tasks to monitor progress.

Do children enjoy this subject?
- The children love reading and bookmaking.
- As staff are getting more ideas and are becoming more enthusiastic, the children are growing further in confidence and enjoyment in other areas.

What types of extra-curricular activities/homework are there in this subject?
- Every child takes home a reading book of their choice three times a week.
- We run a book making club and our Y6 children and parents have been involved in producing a community newspaper.
- Homework is left to teachers' discretion.

How do you support other teachers' planning in this subject?
- Alongside the Permanent Plan, teachers have a planning grid for each half term. It focuses on a specific genre of literature; fairytales, poetry etc. Each focus has a senes of writing opportunities linked to it.

FIG 14.1
(cont'd)

How do you help other staff with their teaching in this subject?

■ I am open and cooperative when staff ask for help and ideas. I also send an informal questionnaire to staff asking about strengths, weaknesses and concerns. I have also worked in other classes and taught poetry writing in the Y6 Intensive programme.

In what ways is parental involvement a feature of this subject?

■ Parents are welcome into school at all times. I am also hoping to invite parents to become part of a 'Parent Pool'. They will be trained in teaching children reading skills and will work alongside teachers in setting up our Reading Tree.

What developments are you planning in the subject?

■ The Reading Tree is the main project at the moment
■ In addition, I am planning a Family Reading Project in liaison with Pennywell School and producing a second community newspaper after the success of the first one.
■ I hope to resource classrooms with listening stations and aim to provide staff with new schemes and ideas to complement the Reading Tree.

What types of documentation are available to staff?

■ There are policies in school on each AT as well as a Spelling Support Pack and a Higher Order Reading Skills Pack. Each member of staff has their own copies.

How is the subject assessed/recorded and reported?

■ I meet with team leaders termly to discuss and monitor the subject. Staff meetings provide the opportunity for feedback.
■ I collect samples of work and set whole school assessments. Each child has a portfolio containing samples of work from Yr3 to Yr6 and a reading record for each half term.

How are assessments acted upon?

■ Assessments are moderated in year group meetings and kept in the team's moderation file. I take samples for my file to analyse and feedback to staff.

How do you make sure that the curriculum meets the needs of all pupils?

■ Our Permanent Plans are taken directly from the National Curriculum documents.
■ Each AT is divided into Levels 1 to 5. The plans are divided into year groups.
■ The planning works alongside our assessment and moderation across school. Results of this assessment and analysis inform future planning.

Have you been on any courses about this subject?

■ I have attended a GEST English course this year. Also I have been on courses for teaching reading, book making and OFSTED preparation for the subject.

FIG 14.1
(cont'd)

What is the status of this subject in the SDP?

■ Funds were available for the Reading Tree. Other subjects are taking priority at the moment however English was of top priority for a long time.

■ Focuses have been added as a result of assessment analysis, such as handwriting and spelling.

What supports/hinders the development of your subject?

■ Staff enthusiasm and cooperation, funding, children's responses to initiatives, liaison with outside agencies, my headteacher's vision and awareness of my own professional development support my subject's development.

Anything else you wish to tell us about?

Please bring along to the meeting, anything that you think will help us understand your subject better e.g. children's work, planning sheets, assessments, photographs etc.

After the inspection

Many schools talk of being in the doldrums after inspection, feeling flat, a bit let down, a bit of an anti-climax. That is understandable if the inspection has been the big thing, the pressure, the target, the goal, and the be all and end all for a year. It is best if it does not assume such importance, but for some schools it does. Maybe, second time around, it will be kept in proportion a little better.

Nevertheless, it is good to plan to 'beat the blues', rather than be caught out. Within the subject, momentum can stop and all the good ideas dry up, so how can we plan to keep things going?

Beating the blues? . . . start before the inspection

Recognising it might happen is a start. Why get caught out or hope it won't occur? Just plan to avoid it. Predict what the inspection will be like: second guess what the team will say, the good points, the low points and the misjudgments you anticipate. Then have a session where everybody in school tells everyone else. Write it down, put it in the safe, get it out after the inspection and say, 'Told you so' or otherwise.

Plan what is going to happen after the inspection. In some schools there is a slow down because everyone is waiting for everyone else to react. Of course, there is the action plan, but that takes 40 days after the report, which takes 7 weeks, so it is a long while before we have to do anything; no wonder things get slow! Plan something to happen in the curriculum while you are waiting for the report, if you don't, it is like waiting for the results of the X-ray and not daring to walk in case the leg is broken.

Plan to take the initiative and be active during the inspection. You will feel better afterwards if you have been involved rather than if you have 'had it done' to you. Get ready for the inspectors, decide what you want them to see, show them, tell them, ask them, be involved.

Plan to hold some important events in school soon after the inspection. Whether it is an educational visit, a poet in residence, or a visiting drama group, try to ensure that there is a focus. The empty diary may look attractive but it leads to problems. The same applies to the date when the report is expected; keep it in proportion by having other things to focus upon.

Beating the blues . . . as the inspection ends

Have a party if you must. So many schools plan a party. That is OK but what can you talk about? OFSTED inspection! Maybe people want a quick chat and then return to normality in their lives. How about a party on the Friday before the inspection, or when the report arrives?

In the longer term it is a good thing to work together on the feedback necessary to different groups involved. The staff, the parents, the governors, the LEA, or the children might need feedback on the inspection. If you work together on it there will be a real purpose in the work.

Have other priorities planned to move the school on quickly. Get into the detailed planning for that drama group, that visit, or that poetry workshop. Recognise that other things matter.

Most important, though, record some good inspection experiences. It is so easy to be negative and tell horror stories. Record your own good things and ask staff for theirs, particularly about English. Make a list, put them on the wall, talk about them.

Beating the blues . . . afterwards

Look at the English section of the report. Be honest about positive and negative issues. So many people look for the criticisms and miss the compliments. Get the predictions out again: were you right? Talk to colleagues. Remember, if you are the coordinator for English, the issues in the report are not about you; they are about the teaching of English in the school. The comments are about the work of all the staff and the achievement of all the children: all the staff teach English.

As coordinator, take the initiative in working on the action plan and the revised curriculum development plan for the school. Ensure that priorities for English get due attention and a realistic chance of success. Also ensure that other priorities do not push English off the agenda and into a backwater. English, more than any other subject has got to be a vehicle for helping other subjects to develop so there must be involvement.

An OFSTED inspection is a thorough review of the quality of work in the school and the subjects taught. The school can be defensive and have the inspection 'done to it' or it can be positive and forward thinking and see the inspection as a chance to engage in a rigorous professional dialogue. There are all sorts of horror stories about inspection. Just like most horror stories they tend to get exaggerated in the telling. There are endless examples of schools where the inspection process has been positive and helpful, after all, most inspectors are experienced professionals with much to bring to the school.

The process is likely to work best where the school itself takes some of the initiative. To be successful in inspection the school should be confident about its own practice and the routine work with the children. Taking the initiative is part of a coordinator's role in the everyday running of the school, not just as an inspection looms.

The contents of this book are a source of good practice, of ideas, practical advice, theory and research background. Using the book well points the way to good practice in English at Key Stage 2 and provides the confidence necessary for success.

Chapter 15

Influencing classroom practice: getting good things going

One of the main tasks of the coordinator is to find ways to encourage teachers to move their work on in the classroom. A series of reports from Ofsted highlight the fact that many schools monitor and evaluate teaching and classroom practice but then fail to take the necessary step of influencing practice for the better as a result of their evaluation. This can be done by providing documentation or setting targets but the most effective way to get colleagues to try new approaches in the classroom is to show them how things might look and offer reasons for the practice suggested. There are different ways of showing people, including

- showing lessons in action;
- arranging displays for staff, which will also be useful for children, parents and governors;
- leading short in-service sessions.

There is much benefit to be gained from giving people 'models' of teaching sessions to allow them to consider, as a starting point, ways of taking the same approach into their teaching. To do this, either through demonstration or talking colleagues through a teaching session, will raise the questions and offer the examples that help teachers to make sense of the curriculum expectations upon them.

An example of such a session might be provided in the following way, where a class of Year 5 and 6 pupils are being encouraged to consider the differences between the book and the film of the popular novel *Charlie and the Chocolate Factory* by Roald Dahl. Over the last half term, the children have listened to and enjoyed the teacher reading the novel, as the class serial. Having read the book, the class have had the chance to watch the film version on video. The teacher now wishes to encourage the children to write about their preferences.

The aims of the session might be summarised as:
- to encourage the children to highlight the differences between the film and the book;
- to encourage speaking and listening opportunities;
- to teach note-taking skills;
- to enable the children to move towards a written account with confidence;
- to put the children in a position where they can write an account without further support from the teacher.

Charlie and the Chocolate Factory: film/book review: planning a lesson

Progress . . . What do I want them to learn?

- How to compare book and film on same topic (*Charlie and the Chocolate Factory*)
- How to plan a piece of comparative writing
- How to discuss and record ideas

Attainment . . . What do I want them to be able to do?

- Speak and listen to small groups
- Contribute to class discussion
- Prepare note-taking framework/layout
- Record discussion ideas
- Contribute with confidence
- Record the version of the book and the film

Response . . . How do I want them to work?

- Cooperate in groups
- Have ideas
- Listen as a class when expected
- Take part with confidence in class discussions
- Take responsibility for recording

Teaching . . . So how will I organise?

- Structure discussion groups
- Use of board to explain layout of A3
- Time limits for group discussion/short well-managed sessions
- Clarify items for each discussion
- Modelling of process
- State purpose and outcome
- Read extract as conclusion

FIG 15.1

Example of a lesson plan for class discussion

Class: Year 5	Lesson: English	Date:
Content of Lesson:		**Resources:**
To prepare pupils to be able to write a comparison of book and film using: 'Charlie and the Chocolate Factory' as basis		A3 paper

Introduction: (possible reference to previous lesson)

State purpose of lesson (as above)
Divide pupils into groups of 3
Instruct for layout of A3 sheet per group, using blackboard

5 mins

Development (Timing, differentiation, learning objectives for each activity/learning group)

Groups to discuss book/film — to note on bullet sheet.
15 mins *Where book was better/film better or the same.*
20 mins *Visitor to each group to explain decisions.*
22 mins *Group to highlight one point to offer in class discussion.*
30 mins *Class discussion, chaired by teacher, recording on board.*
Turn over A3 Sheet. Construct new record frames.
31 mins *Groups of 3 record: Questions they would ask the author.*
36 mins *Questions to ask film producer / Best bit in either.*

Conclusion:

Visitors return to own group — discuss suggestions.
40 mins *Identify good examples for class discussion.*
44 mins *Class discussion.*
Remind pupils of purpose — now prepared to write unaided (when asked) about the book and film, using the sheets as planning.
50 mins *Read extract from book suggested as best bit.*

Future development of the subject area

In future lesson pupils write comparison (unaided).

Stage by stage through the plan (Fig 15.1)

Children put into groups of three — each group with one A3 sized sheet of paper and one pencil. Writing to be done by child in the middle.

Introduction — teacher explains that we are going to consider the differences between the book and the film through discussion, therefore a proforma is needed. Each group scribe draws lines on the A3 sheet to divide the sections, add the titles and place bullet points. Time allowed 2 minutes.

Teacher instructions — teacher explains to the children that they can talk in their group of three and offer suggestions about where the book is better, where the film is better or where they are the same (Fig 15.2). Up to four suggestions are allowed in each section.

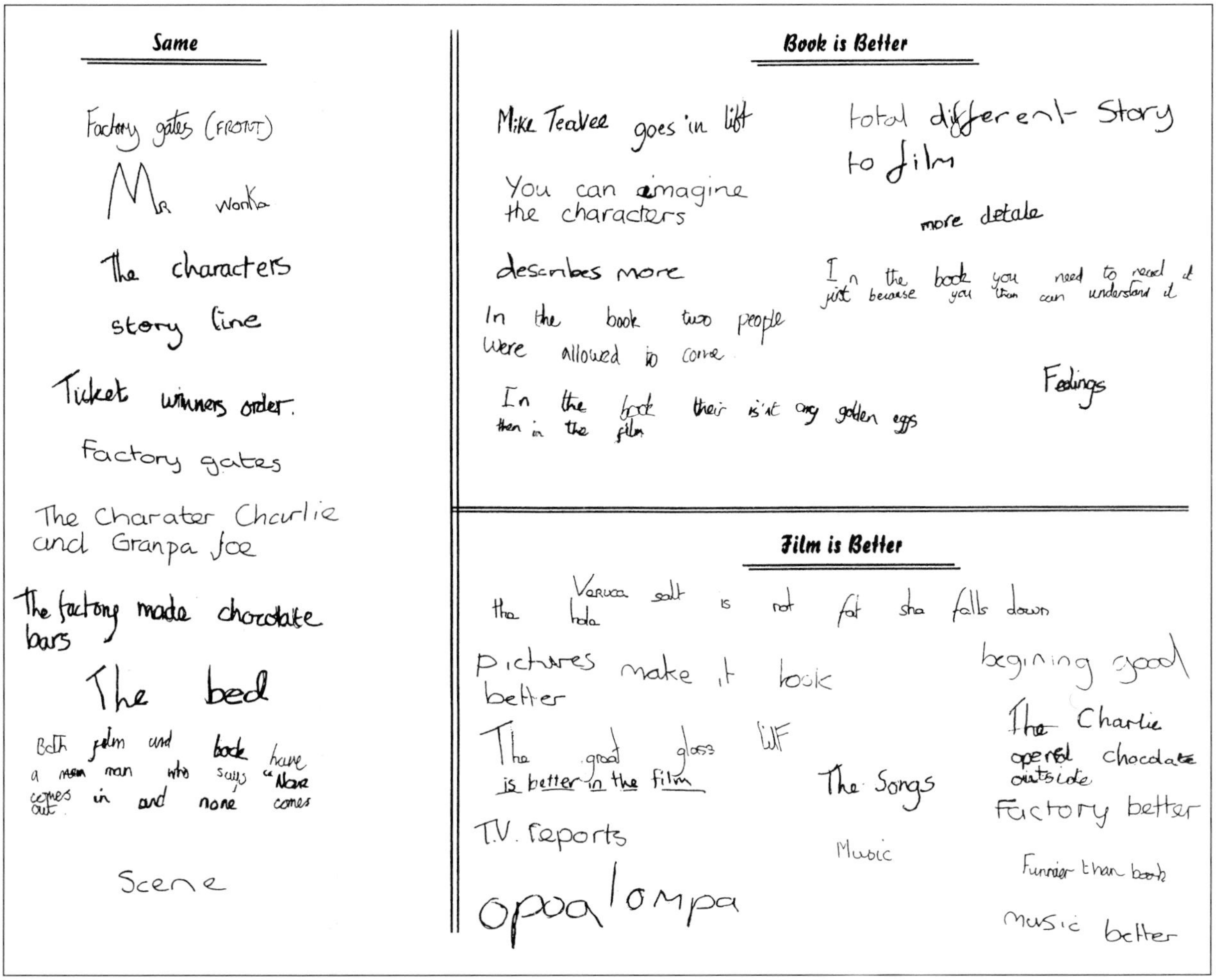

FIG 15.2
A collation of responses

Suggestions are to be recorded in note form, rather than sentences. Time allowed 15 minutes.

Development — children discuss and record, teacher observes, no interaction with groups.

Class instructions — after the 15 minutes the teacher informs children that for all groups to report back separately will take considerable time and there will be much repetition, therefore, in order to find out what another group has said, the procedure will be to take the opportunity to study another group's sheet. Each writer takes A3 sheet and pencil to another group and discusses the responses with the two pupils she visits. Therefore, all children have the chance to discuss their own plus one other group's responses. Time allowed 5 minutes.

Identification of notable points — the teacher asks the two people in each group being visited to identify one point per section on the A3 sheet which will be offered in class discussion. They do this by marking with an asterisk. Time allowed 5 minutes.

Class discussion — teacher leads the class discussion and invites pupils to contribute their asterisked suggestions (Fig 15.3). The teacher fields and develops these ideas and makes notes on the board. Time allowed 10 minutes.

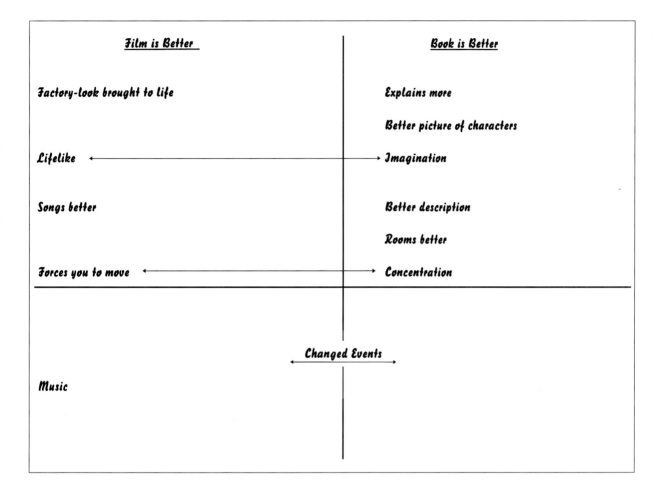

FIG 15.3
Notes on the chalk board

Further discussion — pupils turn over the sheet and complete three new sections:

■ questions they would like to ask the author;
■ questions they would like to ask the film producer;
■ parts of the book that no-one should miss.

Time allowed 10 minutes.

Sharing ideas — teacher instructs 'visitors' to return to their own group and share with their friends the suggestions made by the other group. In this way all groups see two examples, time allowed, 5 minutes.

Summary — teacher asks pupils for their suggestions for each section and fields and develops ideas (Fig 15.4). Time allowed 5 minutes.

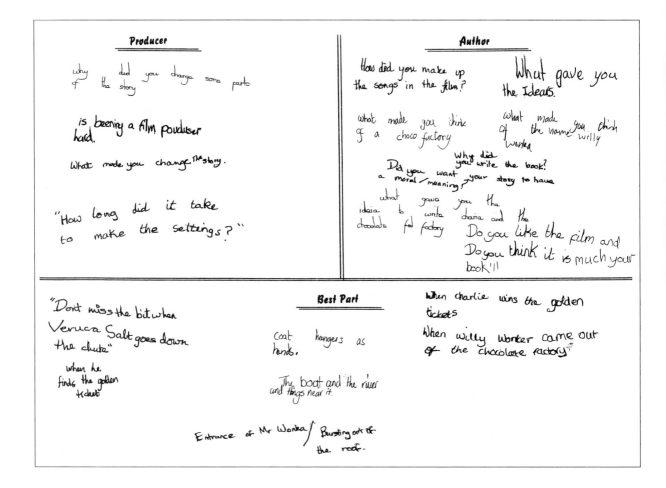

Producer

why did you change some parts of the story

is beening a film pouduser hard.

What made you change the story.

"How long did it take to make the settings?"

Author

How did you make up the songs in the film?

What gave you the Ideas.

what made you think of a choco factory

what made you think of the name willy Wonka

Why did you write the book? Did you want a moral / meaning your story to have

what idaia gave you the to chocolate write diaria and the fat factory

Do you like the film and Do you think it is much your book'll

Best Part

"Don't miss the bit when Veruca Salt goes down the chute"

when he finds the golden tickets

Coat hangers as hands.

and The boat and the river things near it.

When charlie wins the golden tickets

When willy Wonker came out of the chocolate factory

Entrance of Mr Wonka / Bursting out of the roof.

FIG 15.4
Questions to ask: A collation of responses

Conclusion — teacher reviews with children what has been done during the session and articulates the view that they should now be able to write their own summaries of the differences between the film and the book without further support from the teacher. In order to bring the lesson to a pleasant conclusion, one of the suggestions made by the pupils as to a part that should not be missed is read aloud to the group.

The central aims of the session were secure in that pupils were able to develop speaking and listening skills. Further benefits and opportunities were developed as:

■ children were encouraged to take responsibility within the session;
■ children followed a process of planning to use elsewhere;
■ children used and developed important social skills.

Conclusion

This is obviously an example of one pattern of teaching. It is not the only way of organising speaking and listening within the classroom. By offering a range of examples we give teachers more options within their repertoire. We can ask questions like, 'How does this pattern compare with your ways of working?' or 'Do you have different patterns to share with colleagues?'

By giving teachers a sample outline plus examples of pupils' work, it is possible for them to get a picture of 'how things might look in the classroom'. Giving them a picture could be done at a staff meeting or it could be done as part of a written document like this one. Better still would be to invite a teacher into the classroom to see the teaching as it happens. To watch teaching in the raw is one of the best ways of learning. The observer sees the perfect practice with faults, practice that is desperately poor, because we all know that everything can not be perfect all the time. Having the confidence to teach in front of each other is one of the major challenges for the profession, yet it remains one certain way to develop practice.

Being a subject leader means having the nerve to try things with colleagues, working alongside colleagues and in front of them. Have the nerve and have a go.

Helping teachers to see the overall picture: The writing process

One way into the task of helping other teachers to get the 'big ideas' is to develop displays which help both children and teachers throughout the school to engage with them. The expectations from the Literacy Framework can be made explicit in a display and the implications and background can help to draw out the issues and provide a coherence of understanding over the four years of literacy hours and beyond.

As an example we could cover one aspect of writing required within the National Curriculum: Children should learn about the writing process.

Throughout the Literacy Framework there are references to the 'process' aspects of writing. The central elements of teaching children about writing are, that for most of us, there is a process that takes place from having the need to write, to producing the writing, through to reflecting on the activity, all of which are included within the expectations for the Literacy Hour. The use of the notion of the writing process will be extended through 'blocked' activities and through 'linked' teaching in other areas of the curriculum in English and in other subjects.

Within the Literacy Framework, text level work on writing composition refers to aspects of the process in the range for every term in Key Stage 2:

- to generate ideas about a topic by brainstorming . . . Year 3, term 1

- to sequence key incidents by listing, charting, mapping, making simple story boards . . . Year 3, term 2

- to plot a sequence of episodes . . . Year 3, term 3

- to write . . . composing headlines, using IT to draft, edit stories . . . Year 4, term 1

- to fill out notes to connected prose . . . Year 4, term 2

- to use writing frames . . . Year 4, term 3

- to use simple abbreviations in note taking . . . Year 5, term 1

- to convert notes for others to read, paying attention to style, vocabulary and presentation . . . Year 5, term 2

- to draft and write letters for a real purpose . . . Year 5, term 3

- to plan, revise, edit writing to improve accuracy . . . Year 6, term 1

- tailoring writing to presentation . . . Year 6, term 2

- to select the appropriate style and form to suit specific purposes and audience . . . Year 6, term 3

If the expectation is prescribed and the steps outlined, then the task of the coordinator is to help colleagues understand the 'big picture', to help them to get the 'big idea' from which these small sections emerge. For teachers to deliver their own small bites without ever knowing how they fit together will lead to children being able to do a range of specific, prescribed tasks without the understanding of the overall issue.

So let's explore the Literacy National Framework demands and the National Curriculum requirements and come to terms with the 'big idea' behind 'Children should learn about the writing process'.

Children should learn about the writing process

It has already been stated that the writing process is not the same as drafting and that the latter does not mean simply writing in rough, correcting and copying up. There are two ways of approaching this area in KS2:

> Sessions in which children work through the whole process in, say, a morning. They can produce a 'Process Display' which enables the teacher to focus on the different stages through which a piece of writing might pass. The children can then actually see the process taking place as their writing contributes to it.
>
> Using the awareness gained from the 'Process Display' to influence the ways in which children view their writing in general.

Where did our writing come from?

If one of the key learning experiences for children in KS2 concerns the ways in which writing might go through a number of stages in its production, it makes sense to focus on short pieces of writing. The following example was aimed at producing a Cinquain — a five line poem with the pattern two syllables (line one), four syllables (line two), six syllables (line three), eight syllables (line four), two syllables (line five). However, the main aim of the lesson was not the production of

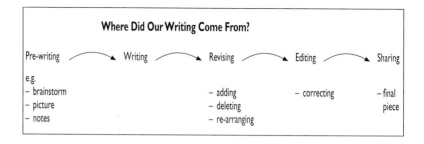

the cinquain but a focus on the writing process. At each stage of the process examples of the children's work were discussed and then added to the display under the appropriate heading. The class was a mixed age Y3/Y4.

Pre-writing

This could be: thinking time
                talking time
                drawing/planning time

Thinking time — There is a great danger of us constantly 'surprising' children with writing. We plan the Monday morning lesson, giving it a great deal of thought, but the children are unaware what is about to hit them! Suddenly they find themselves faced with having to write something. A good idea to establish is that of giving children prior notice. 'Next Monday we are going to be . . .' 'Don't forget on Monday we will be . . .' A week before this lesson the children were told what was going on. A group of primary schools and a secondary school were collaborating on the production of an anthology of writing on the theme of 'Families'. They had a week to think about what they might write.

Talking time — The children were put into groups of three and four to determine what aspect of 'Families' they might write about. Initially there was a brainstorm — two minutes to list anything potentially suitable. Each group had a sheet of sugar paper and large pens so that all members of the group could see what was being listed. Now there was discussion about particular choices. A chance to clarify thinking and gain confidence from having received group approval.

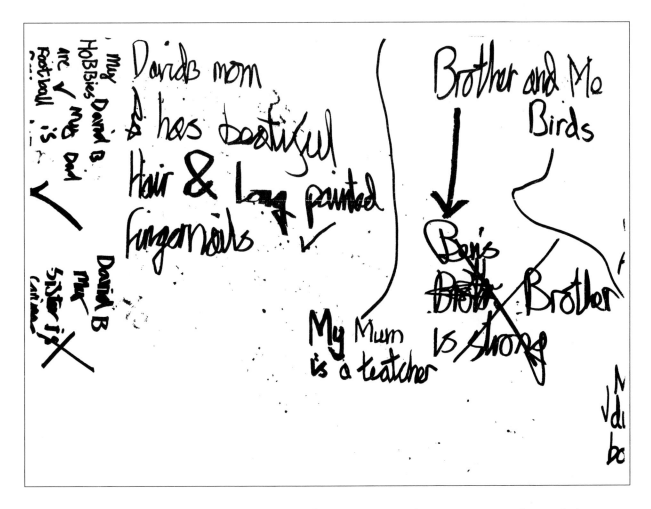

Drawing/planning time — the writing was to be carried out either alone or in a pair with the chance to further discuss and perhaps jot down ideas for a plan — a plan can be words, diagrams or pictures. Some children used the original brainstorm sheet to plan as shown here (one corner)

Some examples of the brainstorms and planning were held up and discussed before being put in place as part of the display.

Writing

Now the children began to write. They knew that these particular pieces of writing were going to be produced in one session and so something short was required. A pair of boys produced:

Pets

My Hamster Likes to escape from the ~~cat of~~ cage. AND comit swarside of the

My cat is black and scears ~~you~~ the living desk

day lights out of you at night.

My birds are dumb and boring because all they do is go tweet tweet.

My Lovebirds are very vishios beaciue they picked one of my budgies to death

My cat likes geting run over. *

* He has got run over 6 times.

Revising

As these pieces were completed the children were advised on how they might revise them. Rather than discuss possible revisions to the original so as to 'improve' them, a particular structure was suggested at this stage which would force children to look critically at their work. They had to convert their writing into only five lines, containing two words, four words, six words, eight words and two words.

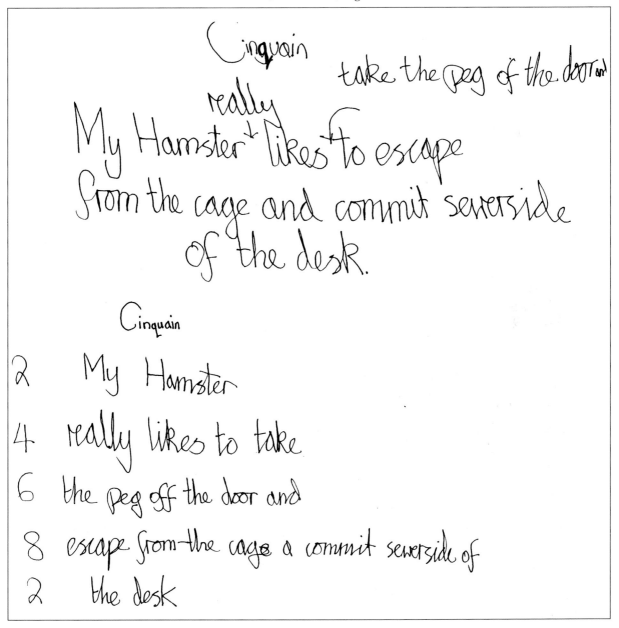

Cinquain

take the peg of the door

really

My Hamster⁺ likes to escape from the cage and commit severside of the desk.

Cinquain

2   My Hamster

4   really likes to take

6   the peg off the door and

8   escape from the cage a commit severside of

2   the desk

Not all children went beyond this stage but some were encouraged to go further and produce a cinquain.

2 My cute

4 Hamster likes to

6 escape from the cage and

8 comit sewerside of the ~~one~~ left

2 desk drawer

My Cute

Editing

Because the work was going to be submitted to an 'editorial board' (and the children knew that not every piece would make the anthology), pieces were corrected through discussion between children and with the teacher.

> My cute
> Hamster likes to
> escape from the cage and
> commit suicide off the left
> desk drawer

The resulting Process Display was very powerful in terms of demonstrating to children what is meant by writing moving through a proces. They were able to compare their first attempt to the final 'crafted' piece. Giving them a structure for their 'revising' enabled them to consider how writing can be improved through redrafting. Such work is an excellent way of developing practice in the teaching of writing in school for it enables all teachers to focus on this area at the same time.

As coordinator you might produce a Process Display with your own class, placing it where colleagues will notice it. It can then be planned as a focus for a particular week during which each class will have a similar session. Reflection on the success of the work and how it has provoked thinking about the teaching of writing makes for an important staff meeting.

'I don't want to!' . . . ownership and writing

Despite the success of the above, we always have to be careful when insisting on such a structured approach to teaching writing and it was a particular Y3 girl who reminded us of the dangers. At the point where children were beginning to be told that they had to revise their writing into the five line structure, she burst into tears. Between sobs she made it quite plain that she did not want to revise her work in this way. Working alone she had produced the following as her first attempt.

A world with different
families

Have you noticed when ever you
go to a friends house they have
a different smell!
Well I have!
I think my family's got a snuggly
warm smell!   It makes you
feel jumpy and excited.
Have you noticed that every
different house has got a colour!
I have!
My familys colour is white and
cream.
It makes you feel comfortable and
happy.
Families also have different seasons!
But not seasons like spring or
autumm
But cheerfulness and caring.
My family's four seasons are

Sharing
Cheerful
Sad
kindness
Have you noticed that every family
has different moods!
I have!.
My family's got a giving mood you
feel godd inside and wanted. my family
has got Different days aswell!
Monday- hectic!
Tuesday- calm!.
Wednesday- happy!.
Thursday- fights.!
Friday -moody!.
The world is full of different families
with different moods.
so next time you go to a friends.
think about how lucky you are
to have a family with different
moods, days, seasons, smells, colours.

In terms of not wanting to redraft this wonderful piece of writing into five lines, she was right! It became the opening piece in the anthology. She felt very deeply about her own work, had ownership of what she was trying to do. It is just this sense of ownership which we need to be aiming at with all children.

Learning from the process display

Discussion of how writing develops through a process should lead to consideration of the part 'process' might play in all of the writing children undertake in KS2. Should it all go through each of the stages discussed above? The key to answering this question lies in the notion of ownership and generally hinges on the decision to move from a draft to a final copy. As teachers we want to use every piece of writing as an opportunity to teach children about writing — to help them improve as writers. This can happen at any stage in the production of a piece of writing, working with an individual child, a group or the whole class. Which children feel the need for an initial brainstorm? Who wants a detailed plan? How could this piece of writing be improved? How could this piece of writing be corrected? While help may be offered at an individual level, all children in a class will benefit from considering how others are approaching the writing and the pros and cons of different ways of working. A piece of writing could then be a rough plan and first draft from both of which the child has learnt a great deal. Whether it needs to be 'copied up' depends — on the original purpose of the writing (for display perhaps or consideration by an 'editorial board' or because the booklet for the child's parents obviously ought to be correct and beautifully presented) — and on what the child thinks. The latter is crucial. We give recognition to the efforts made so far but accept it if the child feels enough is enough. Having said this there are two important considerations:

1 The work produced be kept in a file as something worth keeping. The planning and drafting and writing over and around (perhaps by both teacher an child) is given status.

2 Children who never want to produce final drafts will need working on, especially in terms of writing for different readers, so that they see the need for doing so. This may need insisting upon — sometimes it is the look of a final piece which first convinces children that they are able to produce something worthwhile after all. They have to be made to do it to convince themselves that they can.

Information Technology — word processing

The use of the word processor in the classroom is best discussed when considering the writing process. There are two key points to make:

I Re-drafting is easier when using a word processor

We have already stressed the problems of children having to re-write, in long hand, fairly lengthy pieces of writing. Even if the 'ethos' described above is established so that not every piece moves to a final copy, it can be difficult for anyone to enthuse about having to do so unless the motivation is extremely strong! However, on the screen, amendments and corrections can be made with the minimum of physical effort. Yet still, in many classrooms the word processor is only used for producing the final copy. Not only is this a waste of its potential, it also proves frustrating because children lack the keyboard skills to carry this out quickly (especially if there is only one machine in the classroom). With a minimum of practice any child (or adult!) can type at a speed close to that at which they are composing. If such work is planned as a paired writing session with the typing shared, children can gain access quite regularly and be encouraged to look critically at the writing and realise how easy it is to amend it.

A second idea combines the use of both the word processor and hard copies of the work. This is perhaps the best way of using machines such as palm tops, which are cheap but which display only a limited amount of the text. The following example shows a pair of children composing on screen — then printing out to revise on paper then easily amending on screen. Children seem to enjoy the freedom of actually writing all over their own writing while knowing it will not involve further laborious work.

The writing followed the same process as that described above, the aim being for the children to produce a process display based on the writing of cinquains. Jessica (aged 8) worked with Danielle (aged 7) on a palm top to produce their first description of a chosen animal:

---

cheeths

A big orange cat with big black spots.

Its a wild anmil that eats   meat, **and** tears apart its prey.

It big **sharp teeth** to tear skins, and long legs to run fast after its **prey.**

Its long skiny tail and big body to **pounse** on.

Now the aim was to convert the writing into a cinquain, firstly based around the number of words in each line and then the number of syllables. Each attempt was printed to be worked on both by the children themselves and through discussion with the teacher. Some of the additions and revisions were the result of suggestions by the teacher, whose aim was not just to enable the children to produce a cinquain but to think critically about the quality of the words and phrases they were using.

```
Sharp teeth
A giant cat
It has long legs to run
Its long skiny waveing tail
eats meat
```

```
Sharp teeth
A giant cat
It has long legs to run
Its long skiny waveing tail.
Eats meat
```

```
Sharp teeth

big orange cat

Long legs to run fast on

Long skiny waveing tail Flowing

Eats meat
```

How much easier just to reprint rather than write out the new version each time!

2 The work of every child looks equally professional when printed

Just the look of it can be a great motivating force especially for those who have difficulties with handwriting or who just lack the motivation to write.

Leading in-service for colleagues: Different types of writing for different purposes

Many coordinators worry about leading in-service events for colleagues or making presentations for parents or governors. The person who leads thirty-odd children through a six hour learning session day in day out can come out in a sweat when faced with talking to adults for an hour or so! We worry about falling off pedestals, preaching what we don't always practice, talking down, talking over heads, losing our train of thought and losing control. We think we will appear silly, or embarrassed, pompous, or out of touch with reality. We wonder whether we will seem as though we are preaching someone else's message and deserting our colleagues as we ask them to do yet more on top of their enormous workload. Nearly everyone goes through these sorts of thoughts.

Yet the in-service session, with a relevant agenda and a clear message, well-designed and structured, can do so much to help colleagues to move their practice on and bring policy to life in the classroom.

Most people focus upon the technicalities; the overhead projector, the paperwork, the words they are going to say, and they plan to get through the session with as few problems as possible.

Essential to good planning is the message; what is it that you want your colleagues to know, understand or be able to do at the end of the session? Very much like a lesson for children, we need to think what it is we are going to 'teach' the adults. If we know what we are trying to teach, can we put together a series of points to convey the message or teach the skill or generate the debate? If we can, then we create the 'story' of the session and, armed with this, we can put together a plan which will make the learning interesting. Out of the plan will come the need for resources and equipment but also will come the points where it would be better to use small group discussion to explore issues, to check understanding or demonstrate the issue. There would be other points where it would be better to just tell them, points where you could ask people to look for examples, and points where you could show examples.

In the example that follows the message for the session is that the essentials of writing are purpose, process and audience. If we look at adult life we can explore the essentials of writing and consider the implications for classroom practice. There is the story of the session, offered as 'A week in the life of a writer.' As you read it you will see the points about adult writing have been structured into an order and each point is followed by considering implications for the classroom. Before we think about actually running the in-service session for colleagues or parents we need to get the 'story' sorted out.

As you read through the 'story', think about which bits may be better *told* to the group and which bits would it be better for them to *discuss*.

A useful way to run an in-service session which focuses on the key ideas underpinning the teaching of writing is to consider:

A week in the life of a writer

All of us are writers. Every day for all sorts of reasons and in a wide variety of situations we put pen to paper. The types of writing in which we engage (and don't engage!) are worth considering in terms of what goes on in the classroom. It would be a bit odd to have 'school' writing and 'real, everyday' writing as two totally different activities. Presumably one of our key aims is to teach children so that they will be able to use writing fluently and confidently as adults.

The question to pose is: Think of the week which has just passed. In groups list every time you have done any writing — however 'trivial'.

Lists compiled by adults are usually divided into what they see as three 'categories':
1 **Everyday writing** (which just about all adults carry out) Shopping lists, signatures on cheques, reminder notes, crosswords, birthday cards, postcards, diaries, personal letters, forms.
2 **Work writing** (only if you have a job which requires it) Reports, plans, business letters.
3 **Creative writing** (which very few adults seem to do — or will admit to doing!) poems, songs, stories, plays.

These lists always provoke discussion amongst teachers during which implications for the classroom begin to emerge.

- Writing always has **a purpose** — most of the everyday and work writing is actually used so that the purpose is fairly obvious. A shopping list **reminds** us to buy what we need, a Christmas card enables us **to keep in touch**, a work report will **inform others**, a business letter may **persuade** someone to a particular course of action. However the purpose of some writing is less obvious. Why exactly do some people keep personal diaries as records of their lives? What purposes drive the writing of personal letters to friends or loved ones? And what purpose does the novelist or poet have in mind (apart from trying to make some money!)?

Implications for school: Having a purpose, a need to write, is a major motivating force for children. How often do they write for 'real' purposes? How often do the children see the only purpose being to produce writing for the teacher, rather than the teacher teaching and helping them to produce writing which will achieve particular purposes?

- We always write for someone, **a reader who will read the writing**. Sometimes that reader is oneself as in a shopping list or a diary. At times we might know the reader personally. On other occasions we might not know the person to whom we are writing but we think we know the sort of person they might be — we would normally feel quite comfortable about how to write to another teacher. A newspaper reporter will have an 'implied reader' in mind. We always write with a reader or readers in mind, and this greatly influences how we compose the writing and the sorts of words and sentences we use (It will also influence how concerned we are about the neatness of the piece!). Does the same apply to novelists and poets?

Implications for school: If the teacher is the only reader of the children's writing, they can simply try and produce what they think the teacher 'likes', rather than develop a sense of the needs and expectations of different readers.

- All writing goes through some sort of **a process**. Sometimes that process takes little time or effort: We **think** about what we need from the supermarket, we **write** the shopping list, we **use** it (and then we throw it away!). On other occasions the process takes much more time and effort. A letter of application for a new job which someone wants desperately, might go through the following stages:

   Thinking about how the letter might go (in the bath, the car...)

   Scribbling ideas on a sheet of paper left by the bed for that purpose

   Talking the ideas through with a friend or colleague

   Having a first go at the letter

   Re-reading it the next day and throwing it in the bin

   Having another go

   Re-writing sentences so that the letter sounds better

   Re-structuring by adding, deleting, moving text around

   Showing it to someone for their comments

   Being satisfied with the final product

   Checking for spelling and punctuation

Writing a 'fair copy' which looks polished and impressive

Proof reading

Sending the letter

Implications for school: The word which is now used to describe the writing process is **drafting**. Yet the above description of the letter of application demonstrates clearly that drafting is only a part of the process. In some schools drafting is still seen as no more than 'write it in rough, correct it and then copy it up'. For children inflicted by this particular process, writing at length has become something to be dreaded (and avoided!) rather than enthused about: 'When my dad was at school he only had to write everything once, now we have to do it twice'. The writing process and the part played by drafting in it have already been discussed in Chapter 1.

■ Some writing is viewed as **'creative writing'**.

Implications for school: We believe that the term 'creative writing' is a problem in schools and classrooms and that it would be better if we did not use it (there is no mention of it in the National Curriculum!). We have two reasons for holding such a view:

1 In school it is generally used to refer to the writing of stories and poems. The implication is that only these two forms of writing are in fact 'creative', so that other forms e.g. letters or reports are not 'creative'. However, all writing of a text where the writer is being careful about the choice of words and sentences is a creative act. A text is being 'created' which will express exactly what the writer is trying to communicate. The above letter of application will certainly be an example of creative writing! We would be far better approaching work in schools in terms of teaching children to write different types of writing. Stories are different from poems which are different from letters. Each of these will involve different layouts and the use of written language in different ways.

2 The term 'creative writing' still carries with it a great deal of bags and baggage from the past when it was used as part of a reaction to teaching which was seen to focus almost exclusively on skills such as spelling and punctuation and grammar. In many classrooms when children wrote in creative writing lessons they were told that such skills did not matter. Still today this rather odd notion has survived, so that in some lessons children are told not to worry about spelling — while in others it seems to matter a great deal! In fact whether spelling matters or not is nothing to do with the type of writing. It is far more to do with when it matters in the process of composition. Look back at the letter of application — at what point does spelling first matter?

■ Most adults (including teachers!) write very little! By this we mean, again, writing where the choice of words and sentences really matters.

If we focus on stories and poems, it may be many years since some teachers actually wrote in these ways (perhaps not since they were at school themselves!). It does seem strange that we might find ourselves trying to teach children how to write successfully in ways we have rarely, if ever, attempted ourselves. In fact the moment an adult sits down to write a poem or a story they are faced with exactly the same difficulties faced by many children. Not necessarily in terms of spelling or punctuation of course, but in how to write the best words in such a way as to express what we want to say. We can learn a great deal about how best to help children learn to write by trying to write something ourselves. We are not advocating teachers spending their evenings and weekends writing poetry! Actually, the best time to do some writing is in the classroom, in front of the children, as they are attempting the same task themselves. This is a powerful teaching strategy which should form a regular part of the KS 2 English curriculum. Through having the chance to observe their teacher trying (and hopefully struggling!) to write a story children will have something on which to **model** their own writing behaviour. Being able to discuss this and reflect on 'how writers write' will add further to the learning.

Considering the ways in which adults write has, then, important implications for how we can approach the teaching of writing at KS 2. These implications focus on three key ideas which should underlie the practice we are trying to establish in the KS2 classroom.

Children should write for a range of purposes

How many purposes are there for writing? Given time, a group of teachers would come up with a very long list — far more than could be covered at Key Stage 2! Some important ones are lists of purposes.

A list compiled for Key Stage 2 can then be organised in terms of when each purpose might be covered over the four years. Some purposes (e.g. writing to narrate a story or to record work which has been completed) will be encountered on more than one occasion, perhaps returned to many times so that children develop their ability to deal successfully with this purpose. To each purpose can be attached types of writing which are distinguished by different characteristics e.g. letters or poems so that children learn about these characteristics as they engage with them. As they write different types for different purposes so they develop an awareness of the different ways in which written language is used on each occasion — the language of poetry is not the same as the language of the report.

Children should write for a range of readers

In addition we work to enable them to develop a **sense of audience** — the likely needs of the intended reader of the writing. The National Writing Project suggested four potential audiences:

■ **The writer** — Children need to have the opportunity to write for themselves, perhaps most importantly to sort out what they think they have learnt. 'Learning logs' and 'think books' enable children to reflect on their own learning and sort out the questions they need to ask. This piece of writing from a Y7 girl makes the point beautifully.

Hazel — Y7

Journals are useful. Mostly I write thoughts in it and questions. Journals are hard to get into because you have to think how to put your thoughts into words and sentences that someone else can understand. Once I start writing (eventually) thoughts and questions continue to flood into my head. The way the teacher answers the questions is good but I think some questions cannot be answered because maybe the teacher doesn't know the answer but guesses or some questions cannot be answered in words but in action. I think you should have one journal and write about and ask questions to individual subject teachers. In the Infants and Juniors we should have had journals because I could think better and quicker then and also had more questions.

- **Other children** — A class of thirty children contains twenty-nine potential readers to whom and for whom a child could write. Across a school the potential is enormous!

- **Known adults** — Of course the teacher will be one of these known adults but perhaps the largest group of potential readers is that of the children's parents. As was pointed out above in the discussion of purposes, it is a very different challenge for a child to write a booklet for her mother describing the science work rather than just 'writing up' the science in an exercise book or file. Mother has not been present during the lessons and the so the child is faced with how to produce something which clearly describes what took place and what was learnt. In so doing the child is forced to sort out her own thinking first — a key element of learning.

Another nice example of writing for parents comes from schools in which children (perhaps working with the headteacher) help to write any newsletters. Some schools even produce regular newspapers, ensuring that *all children* are expected to be involved at different times;

- **Unknown general audience** — the world beyond the child's immediate life can be used as an audience for writing when children write articles for local newspapers or request information from companies. The following letters were written following a walk to the 'park' which adjoined Mortimer Road Primary School, South Shields.

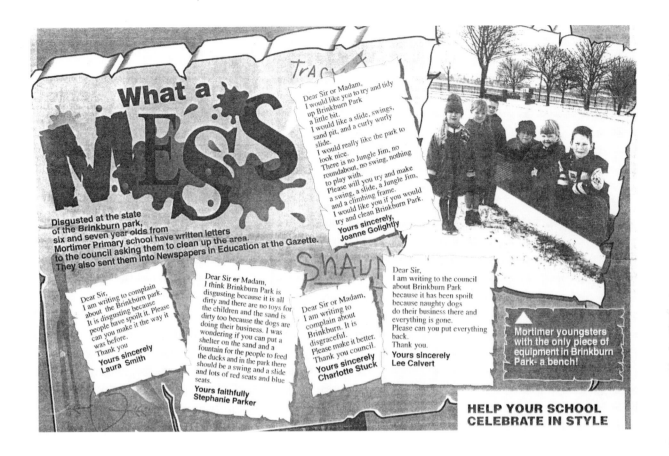

It is important to remember that the drive to find purposes and readers for children's writing is not just to give them the chance to write for people other than the teacher. The key teaching and learning in this area involves a developing knowledge of the different ways written language can be expressed and organised depending on the format, the purpose and the likely reader. Again the reading/writing connection is fundamental — children need to read written language used in these ways if they are to write successfully. We learn to write by reading as much as writing.

As you have read the 'story' of the session you will have seen the message unfold. The message is the summary of the whole thing. It should fit in with the school policy on, in this case writing, and it will be something, which, by working through the session you should be able to have demonstrated.

You may then wish to show how this fits in with curriculum expectations from outside the school. The Literacy Framework states that

- writing is closely related to reading;
- pupils need to understand that their writing will be read by different audiences;
- pupils need to see the process being modelled by the teacher.

Showing the list above could conclude or open your session or both. Working through the story takes the 'big idea' within the National Curriculum and the Literacy Framework and makes sense of it within the context of everyday life so that teachers can see the relevance of the school policy and the wider aims of the school.

Returning to the 'story' of the session, it should be possible to plot which bits need to be *told* to staff. The implications for school can be envisaged as the parts where teachers listen to you as you present some points. The parts leading up to each of these implications are opportunities for teachers to engage in *discussion*. Staff can be placed in small groups to consider the key questions. By chatting about each bit in order they will be led to the key issues and the implications for school in a way which is relatively efficient in terms of time, avoids discussion which is too wide ranging and difficult to draw together, and keeps everyone involved.

So now we can think about timing. The group discussions need only be short, say five minutes, maybe allowing a further five minutes to compare with other groups. The implications for school can take five minutes each, with perhaps a further three minutes for groups to chat about their reactions to the points made.

What is now emerging is a balanced session, with time for group work, time for exposition by the leader, some activity, some listening; so similar to a good lesson for children!

The rest fits in with what has been decided. If a group is going to make notes about *discussion* then the group needs big sheets of paper and pens. It needs an appropriate space, so move the chairs. It needs to be the right size, say three people, and it needs time limits. For the parts where the leader is *telling* the group things, then everyone needs to be able to see without moving chairs, you might need a prepared transparency on a screen, which means you need to know how to work the overhead projector. Alternatively you might just write key points on a big piece of paper.

There you have it: a planned piece of in-service training for staff around one of the 'big ideas', bringing in key aspects of the National Curriculum and the Literacy Framework. All you need now are the essentials; things like refreshments, heating and a clear idea of how you are going to start and finish so that real purpose is communicated.

The 'story' above can be worked through in one hour. You might use the examples given or provide your own. To plan other sessions just select another 'story' to tell and go through the same process. The stories can be taken from elsewhere in this book or from particular questions you need to answer in your school. You might have a whole day to fill, so use three stories rather than stretch out one over too long a time span.

If you work in this way you will be sure that
■ you have something relevant and important to say;
■ that the message makes sense;
■ that the structure will keep people involved;
■ that the organisation will flow.

You will be confident and assured and less nervous. You could talk it through with a colleague beforehand or, better still, involve them in the running of it. What is certain is that a lot of the worries about what other people will think are often unfounded. Colleagues are usually highly delighted that someone else is running the session and someone else has done all the planning!

Part five Resources for learning

| Chapter 16 | Setting a budget |

Setting the budget has become one of the jobs of the subject leader that appears on the job description, turns up in all the papers from the Teacher Training Agency, and is part of most courses on doing the job. It is one of the tasks that is a worry to many new coordinators. The truth is that it is not that much of a worry because in most schools the budget is not very big! However much there is to spend, though, it is important that it is spent correctly and that agreed systems are understood by everyone concerned so that the reasons behind allocations and decisions are clear. Every school is different which makes it impossible to give a stereotype model for the fixing and spending patterns associated with setting a budget, however, we can think through the various phases of the process to apply to our own situation and a model might be helpful.

Setting a budget is a case of working through a series of stages, step by step, in order to ensure you get the best value from the limited amount of financial resources available. It is a bit like planning a holiday; there are things you would like to do and there are limits to what you can afford. You have to select the destination that allows you most of the experiences you want within your price range.

How much is there to spend?

You cannot plan a budget properly until you know how much there is to spend. In most schools the amount available for spending on resources and equipment is about 5 per cent of the total budget for the school. After the costs of staffing, premises and other overheads are identified, the amount remaining is that which can be spent upon the curriculum subjects. There are alternatives which governing bodies should consider even if it means asking awkward questions about priorities. This may lead to unpalatable decisions but the governing body has a duty to consider which proposals will offer best 'value for money' to the school.

What are the priorities?

Having the money is fine but spending it without a plan is not efficient and this is where a budget becomes important. Just like the child with pocket money who blows it all on sweets or spends it all in the first day, the coordinator has to balance priorities and ensure that there is some sense of order about the way the money is allocated:

- **It has to last the year.**
- **It has to give value for money.**
- **It must meet a need.**

In order to ensure spending is appropriate the coordinator for English needs to work with the staff and the senior management of the school to identify priorities. On an annual basis it is necessary to carry out an audit of the quality of work in English. The issue of doing an audit is dealt with on pp. 00–00. The coordinator has the picture of needs from within the school, from the work of the children, results of assessment, from staff questionnaires, from SEN statements and perhaps a post-OFSTED inspection action plan. The senior management bring a picture of other needs and possibilities such as LEA initiatives, the expectations of the Literacy Framework, opportunities for partnerships, and funding from other sources. Figure 16.1 outlines the influences upon school priorities.

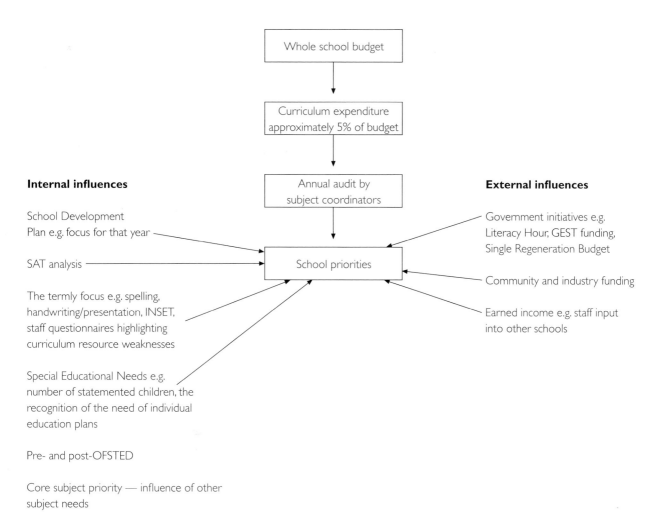

Whole school budget

Curriculum expenditure approximately 5% of budget

Annual audit by subject coordinators

School priorities

Internal influences

School Development Plan e.g. focus for that year

SAT analysis

The termly focus e.g. spelling, handwriting/presentation, INSET, staff questionnaires highlighting curriculum resource weaknesses

Special Educational Needs e.g. number of statemented children, the recognition of the need of individual education plans

Pre- and post-OFSTED

Core subject priority — influence of other subject needs

External influences

Government initiatives e.g. Literacy Hour, GEST funding, Single Regeneration Budget

Community and industry funding

Earned income e.g. staff input into other schools

FIG 16.1
Illustration of needs

Setting the budget

With all the different priorities being presented from all the coordinators, the challenge of setting the budget lies ahead. It is a case of give and take, presenting the best case, compromising and agreeing the best way to share out a finite amount in the best interest of the children's learning. In some schools the head goes away and prepares the budget and tells all coordinators how much they can have to spend. In others, the head tells nobody how much there is and tries to keep spending low for an end of year 'feel good' flourish: Elsewhere, the favoured few get what they want and others do not get what they need. With the oversight of the governing body in finance, it should be difficult for these practices to continue but heads who do not itemise subjects in curriculum spending can still operate in these ways unless a governor asks for detail.

The best way forward is for the staff together to reach agreement on the balance of priorities. If each coordinator presents their priorities and reasons to everyone else the chances of open communication and understanding are greater. The presentation of information does not have to be onerous; a simple school proforma, used by everyone to identify priorities and calculate proposed spending helps everyone to see the decisions each has reached. This allows for a better, more open debate about the priorities, the balance of spending and decisions. Agreements then, really are agreements and some of the problems of patronage and favouritism are avoided.

The school needs to be sure of its long-term plans to ensure that 'dedicated' funding is secure. For example, if the school wants to ensure that the library serves its purpose in developing reading then it will need to grow and develop over time with money 'dedicated' to it in the longer term. It is not possible to build a good library in one go: it is not worth allocating money one year and not the next.

As a result of agreeing priorities it is obvious that some needs are not met and the school needs to consider these and agree some contingencies in the budget. If by chance additional funding does become available, what are the spending priorities which will come forward? If this agreed at the outset time is saved later.

'Spending it'

If the best systems are used to identify priorities and set the spending totals, it should be possible to give the coordinator control over the spending. There should be no need to refer to management for permission as spending should operate on the basis that if it is needed, buy it because it was on the plan and it will address the priorities we agreed. The coordinator should be able to justify spending by referring to the agreed budget.

Systems are needed to give the coordinator the information necessary to be efficient in spending. With computers to do the work the coordinator should only need to cast an eye over progress regularly and to check that spending is on target. Since a lot of spending should take place early in the year, the rest of the budget will trickle along rather than flow: Intermittent checks should be made, but at this stage, it is a case of monitoring the spending rather than the budget. Agreements about the use of the money have already been made and issues to do with value for money and effectiveness of spending should not arise if people stick to agreements made.

Of course budgets sometimes change, occasionally for the better! Schools can get windfalls. It could be that local business and industry links bring in funding for a specific local initiative which provides wider opportunities than those envisaged. Similarly, with a post-OFSTED inspection grant, whilst the money comes only once at a specific time, the date it is due and the amount that will be available is known. The overall budget can be adjusted to cover the action plan but careful thinking and strategy by senior management at the stage of sorting out will have identified the possible contingency arrangements, taking account of the key issues for action identified.

In some schools a small amount of curriculum money is held back for unforeseen spending. The senior management team can back up developments and ensure that crises are avoided by operating a limited fund to support good ideas, particular children's needs or make things happen that would otherwise have been missed for the lack of a small amount of money. For instance, a newly arrived pupil with an individual education plan that cannot be covered from existing resources might benefit enormously in a new school from the allocation of the money to buy some particular materials. A 'special offer' from a publisher to buy 'three for the price of two' might be too good to miss and help to meet known needs for next year as well as this — so spending now will save money in the long term.

The number of exceptions are all examples of strategies that make the logic of the budget unclear. However, there does need to be a clear process in school to help the coordinator manage this important part of the job.

Checking it was spent wisely

A key to efficiency relates to checking on the way money is spent. Efficiency means 'value for money' and it is important to check that decisions about spending were good ones for the implications can be considered in the future.

The central question is whether the spending made a positive difference to children's achievement. The achievement does not have to be measurable. It might be demonstrated in terms of improved results, higher reading scores, however, it could also be demonstrated in terms of the level of borrowing from the library, children's interest in books or the improvement in the quality of writing because children are exposed to better quality texts.

Before the budget cycle starts again it is useful to be able to demonstrate the impact of the last decisions. To do so justifies the spending, checks on progress, but also makes the budget process viable.

Chapter 17   Effective use of resources

Setting a budget and building up suitable resources is an essential part of the co-ordinator's job. Good resourcing is more than getting the catalogues, selecting items, doing the budget, and ordering and distributing stock. Resourcing is the practical end of the policy, where principles become routine and the right materials are used in the right way. Effective use of resources is difficult to achieve. We can publish guidelines and hope people take note or we can suggest ways to develop effectiveness.

In all subjects there are two key areas where resourcing is a real challenge:

- getting colleagues to 'know' their materials, what they can do, and how to use them — in English this is, most significantly, the books.

- to organise shared areas so that children can run them and staff set consistent expectations — in English this is the library.

Teachers need to 'know' their resources

Throughout the Literacy Framework there is emphasis upon the range of fiction, poetry and information texts that children should meet and work with in order to develop the required levels of literacy. The Literacy Framework expects sessions on guided reading, shared reading, independent reading, silent reading. It also expects the teacher reading to the class and pupils' own reading for interest and pleasure, which should take place outside of the literacy hour. For teachers, this means more work, not less. Teachers need to know the texts and then know which ones will work best for which children in which circumstances.

One of the major challenges for Key Stage 2 teachers is developing knowledge of the books children will be reading i.e. finding the time to read the books on the shelves in the class or school library. Yet surely we ought to know. If we have not read the books ourselves we are unable to advise children and unable to inspire them through our own enthusiasm. A reception teacher can take home thirty books from the reading corner and in one evening familiarise herself with all of them. She will then be able to manage their use in the classroom. Just considering novels in Y6, whether from one of the latest schemes or the local bookshop, involves books with over one hundred pages each. This really is an important issue because we would argue that the biggest single in-school factor influencing the amount of reading children undertake at Key Stage 2, and their attitude towards reading, is the knowledge and enthusiasm of the teacher. As a coordinator you need to consider how to instil this knowledge and enthusiasm in staff who may have read very little children's fiction or poetry or non-fiction and who consider they have more than enough to do without being asked to spend evenings and weekends reading such books.

This may appear to be an insoluble problem for the coordinator but there is a way of tackling it through one of the key opportunities which teachers can offer to children so that they read at school. It gives the coordinator the chance to influence classroom practice, establish a whole-school approach and develop the knowledge of teachers all at the same time! The aim is to ensure that children engage in some form of structured reading activity every day — maybe a week on one approach or different days for different approaches.

Different reading strategies

For many years regular sessions of **silent reading** in class (ERIC or USSR or whatever) have been suggested because they are good for the children. We certainly view such sessions as one important element of lessons, during which children read for a sustained length of time, although there are other elements which are discussed below. But we would argue that silent reading is best viewed as being for teachers rather than children! The key is that teachers use the time to read children's books. In terms of fiction, you need to provide your staff with a starter list of authors and titles (see Chapter 18) which they will read. Three such sessions a week of twenty minutes each, means an hour a week, twelve hours a term, thirty-six hours a year. Some books will be skimmed. Others will so hook a teacher (for many of them are an excellent read) that they will be taken home without you having to suggest it! Within a year it is possible to achieve a situation in which all the Key Stage 2 staff have achieved a good basic knowledge and the children know that they have. In addition, the children have observed their teachers reading and enjoying the books. Regular silent reading should lead to a few minutes considering what has been read over the twenty minutes. Children can discuss their reading in pairs or small groups. Some can tell the whole class. The teacher can enthuse about what she has been reading and perhaps read an extract as a 'taster' to tempt children to read the book. Recommendations can be made as well as plans for future reading. An ethos is established within which all the class — children and teacher — enjoy reading and discussing what they have read. We must never underestimate the power of such a simple approach. Teachers faced with classes of reluctant readers may be cynical at first, and the hardest challenge will be getting them started (the teachers!), but the effects are almost always dramatic.

We certainly do want children to consider more challenging texts containing the features listed in the National Curriculum and to engage in work to help them learn about these features. But if they are just doing this work, without any real enthusiasm, it is hard work for all of us. First and foremost we want to get children reading, wanting to read and enthusiastic about it.

In addition to regular sessions of silent reading there are other activities which should be planned to enable children to read for a sustained length of time. The two most important are **paired reading** and **group reading**. In both cases texts can be chosen which the children concerned are able to read without much help — the enjoyment comes from reading *with* a friend or a teacher or a parent. However, they have another important use in that we can set them up for children to attempt to read something they either could not or would not attempt alone. Two readers can help each other through a book which neither could read alone. We should aim to establish a whole-school approach whereby every day a child will spend some time engaged in one of these three.

Paired reading

There are many useful variations of paired reading but all involve the same basic principles — two readers reading aloud together, helping each other if necessary and feeling free to discuss whatever turns up in the text. In the 'basic' version one of the readers is less advanced and will be helped through the text by the partner, so it could be an adult with a child, an older child with a younger child or two children of the same age but different reading abilities. One of the pair begins reading, both knowing that the reading has to be shared. Should the less advanced reader begin to struggle, a nudge from her partner means the reading will be taken over and she can follow the text as it is read to her. However she knows that she is expected to take over herself when she feels confident. Again a nudge signifies her intention to do so. The two readers work through the text with regular nudges and regular pauses to respond to what has been read.

Variations on this idea will depend on the type of pair (ability/mixed ability/friendship) and the level of difficulty of the text for both readers. They can include the following:

■ Taking it in turns to read alternate paragraphs or alternate pages. This is especially useful to consider for parents of Key Stage 2 readers who may consider their responsibility to do some reading with their children to be over now that they have 'learnt to read'. Schools frequently find it difficult to sustain parental help with older children, especially if the reading books simply continue to go home as they have done since the child first started school. Alternate pages are great fun and there are many examples of parents continuing the practice to GCSE as the only way of ensuring their child actually reads the English Literature set novel! Teachers and parents need to have explained to them that they are in fact doing more than simply share the reading. Through the ways in which they read their pages — their intonation, pace, pauses — they are **modelling reading** to the child, demonstrating that this is how the text has to be read. The aim is for the child to pick up features of the adult's reading and begin to use them herself. The ways in which adults can model aspects of the English curriculum for children must never be underestimated as a powerful teaching strategy. There is a danger that because it is such a simple notion we do not explicitly recognise its potential.

■ The more advanced reader reads a paragraph or page first and then the child reads the same paragraph or page. This is especially useful for struggling readers when we want to help them through a text which is too difficult for them to read alone. The adult reading provides the child with a 'map' of the text. Not only have 'difficult' words been read (so that when the child encounters 'yacht' she knows that this peculiar looking word is 'yacht' because it was 'yacht' when the adult read it!) but, perhaps more importantly, a 'map' of intonation has been established which is the most important map of all. This version of paired reading can be extended to involve the reading of the page first, then both readers reading the page together in unison, followed by the child having a go on her own. Whether the page is read in unison will depend on the difficulty of the text for the child. Where such sessions are a regular part of the struggling readers' reading curriculum (whether at school or at home), children are able to tackle texts which have more demanding vocabulary and more complex sentence structures than are contained in the books specially written for them. If they are never to meet such texts there is little chance of them bridging the gulf which separates them from 'real reading'. In addition these texts have 'status' in their eyes and the eyes of their peers, thus helping to raise the self-esteem of the child condemned to choosing what they call 'thin books'. On seeing the child clutching Roald Dahl's *The Magic Finger* a friend might well comment 'I've read that. It's good isn't it?' Such moments can be a powerful motivating force for a child to continue grappling with reading. Finally, this strategy enables struggling readers to participate in any silent reading sessions because they are able to re-read the pages read in a pair, silently to themselves.

Group reading

Like paired reading this strategy is all about children helping each other through a text.

The most common approach is for groups of three or four children of roughly the same reading standard to work together. Again, once the children have established how to manage the activity for themselves texts can be chosen which 'stretch' them as readers. Such 'stretching' could refer to vocabulary, sentence length and structures, text structures or simply length! Tackling for the first time a 'really thick book' (as one child said) is often easier in a group than on one's own. However, group reading is not to be confused with that activity which so many of us suffered as children and which now, thank goodness, has just about expired — reading round the class. Anyone having been exposed to this will remember the desperate looking ahead as we tried to predict which passage we would have to read when it was our turn (while not taking any notice of the passage actually being read at the time!) and the awful dread of getting stuck in front of all one's classmates. The crucial difference with group reading is that everyone in the group has to be ready to *help* anyone who gets in a muddle or gets stuck. All members of the group have to follow what is being read in order that they will be able to help. Once children realise that getting stuck is OK, and that we all get stuck sometimes, an ethos is established which enables group reading to be an excellent reading activity.

Teachers should, of course, monitor the groups. Once it is established and the groups support themselves there should be little call on the teacher's time, but we can join particular groups if necessary. We may want

- to join in and help a group, modelling the way the text ought to be read through our own reading;
- to encourage children to offer help when someone is stuck;
- to assess a particular child's reading during the session;
- to encourage children to pause and discuss the text, demonstrating through our own comments how readers go about discussing what they read.

During group reading we can do a lot of subtle teaching as well as learn a great deal about children as developing readers.

Guided reading

This is generally silent group reading. Again each child has the same text but now they each read a section silently. Having done so they discuss the text, either with the teacher leading or with an agenda left by the teacher. This can be in the form of questions or discussion points, it depends on the children, the text and the teacher's aims. Guided teaching is a key teaching strategy within the National Literacy Strategy as well as enabling teachers to assess and monitor children.

Reading aloud

Finally we must not forget the most basic teaching strategy: reading aloud to the class. The 'Range' section of the National Curriculum states that children 'should be encouraged to develop as enthusiastic, independent and reflective readers' and a key way in which we can establish enthusiasm (which will lead to 'independence' and 'reflection') is by reading to children. As we shall see there are more benefits to be gained from reading aloud than just the development of an enthusiastic attitude.

Reading aloud has always been a major feature of early years and Key Stage 1 classrooms, yet even here its seems to have been under threat during the past six or seven years (since the introduction of the National Curriculum). Whenever we ask teachers, they always look a little guilty and then speak about all of the other curriculum subjects they now have to 'fit in' to the school week. Teacher reading aloud has suffered because in many classrooms it has been viewed as little more than a treat to end the day. We've worked hard all day so we can finish with a story. This is not the place to discuss in depth the importance of reading aloud from a range of texts in the early years because of the fundamental 'reading lessons' which children learn from these sessions. However, we neglect it at our peril. At Key Stage 2 the activity may be marginalised to an even greater extent if we believe that English teaching is about other activities, however, consider the following research from New Zealand which focused on the effect of reading aloud on the vocabulary acquisition of children (Elley, (1989) 'Vocabulary acquisition from stories' in *Reading Research*, Quarterly, Spring 1989).

The first part of the research was carried out with 157 7-year-olds all of whom were read the same short story in class by their teachers. Before they heard the story, though, they were 'tested' on a set of words which occurred in the text to determine that no child knew the meanings of them. The words were presented orally and children had to point to one of three pictures which represented the meaning. If they could not do so it was assumed they did not know the meaning. The story was then read aloud by the teacher three times in the course of a week. There was no discussion of the meanings of the 'test words', but the story was discussed by the teachers and classes. After a further week each child was re-tested on the words. There was an average 15 per cent increase in their ability to indicate the pictures which represented the meaning of the particular words. The 'low ability' readers made the most gain.

This appears to be a dramatic increase in vocabulary and the researchers decided to repeat it with 127 8-year-olds. This time they used two different stories and varied the lessons. One set of lessons simply repeated the first experiment, with the following results:

Increase in knowledge of meanings of words
Story A	15 per cent
Story B	4 per cent

In the other set of lessons, the teachers were told to read the words as they occurred in the texts but then provide an instant explanation (either another word with the same meaning or a paraphrase) and read on. There was no discussion of the words as such. Results were:

Increase in knowledge of words
Story A   40 per cent
Story B   17 per cent

When asked about any differences between the two stories, teachers said that the children had been more involved in Story A. The most dramatic result, then, was achieved by simply reading aloud a story which the children enjoyed, providing brief explanations of 'difficult' words as they occurred in context — 40 per cent average increase, with the 'low ability' readers making the most gains. In the 'Standard English and Language Study' section of the Reading Programme of Study it states that children should 'develop their understanding' of the vocabulary of standard English. This research suggests that the strategy just described should certainly form part of any work in this area.

Running a school library

If we want children hooked on books, then we have to make books special in school. One place to do this is in the school library.

Most primary schools attempt to provide a library system of some sort. The reasons vary:

- The school library is part of a philosophy — children are growing up in the real world and the real world includes libraries. If schools can instil in children the notion of using a library in the primary school, then they may make use of the wider provision.

- Children develop qualities such as decision making, selecting and sharing as a direct result of experience in using a school library.

221

■ The library is a practical way of organising resources, having a centralised collection available to a wider range of users than a classroom-based resource.

■ It is an aspect of school that children or parents can help to organise and run.

In times of strict financial limits, some schools seem unsure of whether to maintain a central resource or disperse books to each classroom. A classroom-based library, often changing, can be a valuable resource as long as there is consistency of organisation so that children learn skills effectively. If well-organised, a classroom-based system can mirror the pattern of library provision in branches with revolving stock (not literally) and inter-branch loans.

However it is organised within school, either centrally or dispersed to classrooms, there are aspects that can be considered to make the most of the provision of a library. This chapter will discuss a central library resource, but the points will apply equally to libraries in classrooms.

Who is the library for?

If the book collection is one that children are expected to visit to select the books they need and then take them elsewhere to use, it is a browsing area. It might, by contrast, be a place where the books are shelved and children select their books and work nearby — a 'busying' area. Sometimes teachers and children are compromised by the uncertainty about what their library is for and how it should be used. Because an area is designated for reading, there is the feeling that all reading takes place there. Class stories are shared in the area, regardless of whether it is of an adequate size. Children are shoe-horned into the space, jammed into each other, overlapping, uncomfortable and unable to concentrate. It would be good to have a purpose-built, spacious library area but, if it is not possible or there are other priorities, then it is a case of making the best use of available resources and space.

Setting out the books

It is obvious that, if we want children to choose to read, books must be made attractive. The more that books can be shelved so that they are facing outwards, showing the cover rather than the spine, the better. Naturally, many books will need to be shelved, but to display a few at a time on stands, shelves, window sills, in baskets, even in a set space on the floor, will make them into an invitation as opposed to a challenge. Books that are displayed can be collected together as a feature:

- books by a particular author;
- books on a theme — for example, religious festivals, minibeasts or fruit;
- books of a type — such as cookery books or atlases;
- new books in the library — a few at a time;
- poems to read aloud;
- books on topical issues.

As a useful technology activity, children at the older end of Key Stage 2 can design and make simple lean-to bookshelves from sheet hardboard with timber battens and lots of white paint. Alternatively, they can design and invent ways of making book display stands from boxes, cartons, storage drums and so on. Children will create book stands, book stages, books nooks, and book baskets, They can decorate them, display them and evaluate their use.

Using books made by children

In many schools, the making of books by children is part and parcel of the curriculum. The activity fulfils many expectations of the National Curriculum, not just in English and the books become a superb resource for the school's own library. If multiple copies can be made, the authors are rewarded for their hard work, but even a single copy can be valued and used.

Non-book resources

The library provision should include a range of non-book resources such as charts, maps, cassettes, videos, and magazines which form part of the material available centrally, either in the classroom or the school. The Dewey system can be used for classification, but the storage and retrieval systems should be well thought out and manageable for pupils. A shelf for outsize books is essential.

Children's involvement in running the library

Ideally, the children should be very involved in running the library. By learning to organise the system they become more aware of how the system works, a form of learning through experience.

Some of the most disorganised resources, including libraries, exist where there is a clear list of child monitors. Better than monitors are 'specialists'; not just the same thing by a different name, but a group of children who work to become experts and then share their expertise with others.

Ways of encouraging children to learn how to use the library effectively are discussed in Chapter 8. Children can be involved in devising ways to help each other use the resource. For example, the trouble-shooter chart shown on p. 225, produced by Year 5 children, is a real attempt to help others use their central book collection. It helps with the library and it is a lovely example of writing for purpose and audience, using the most appropriate style and presentation.

Many schools ask parents to volunteer to help service the library as a resource. All that has been said about monitors applies to parents. If the parents are seen as people who tidy up and sort things out, children are less likely to bother with keeping their library tidy and well-organised. Adults can be used to work with, rather than working for, children and they may need 'training' in what is expected and how to help.

Naturally, a member of staff must be in overall charge, but the time available is limited by other responsibilities, so finding efficient help is vital. The teacher needs to be able to stand

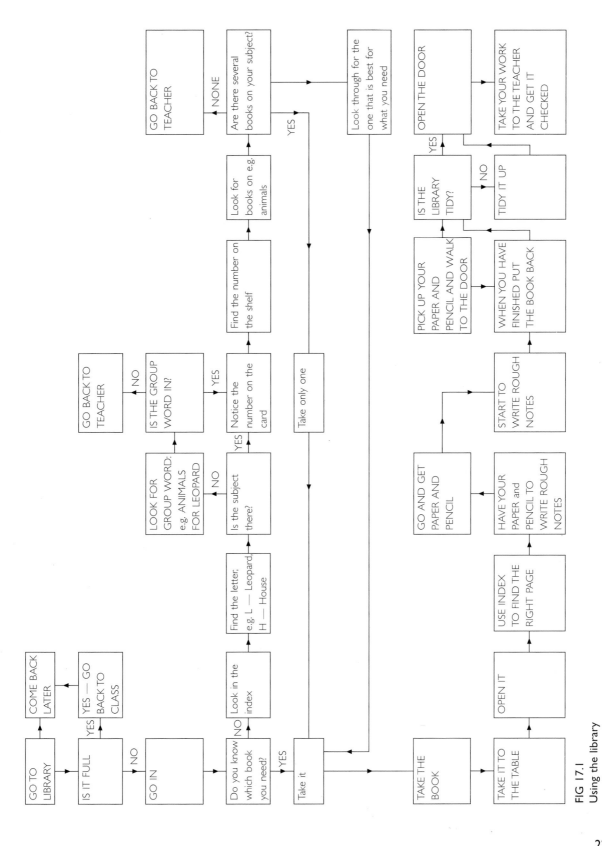

FIG 17.1
Using the library

back and consider whether the library is working in the way it should. They should check whether it is being used by all ages, both sexes and children from all ethnic groups, both from the equal opportunities angle, but also as part of monitoring the effectiveness of the teaching of reading throughout the school.

Ordering Stock

Publishers send representatives and catalogues, but most teachers prefer to see the books as they choose. Library suppliers usually welcome teachers buying books from stock. This gives opportunity for browsing, evaluation and getting the feel of a book. All this helps the teacher to spend limited money with more confidence. Of course, it is preferable to have a shopping list before being confronted by the volume of available stock, as it is easy to spend the allotted amount before seeing all the available books. Knowing beforehand what is required is not just about looking for gaps on the shelves. It may be that a well-stocked section is under-used because the books are not appropriate. This is part of the monitoring task.

Before new stock is purchased, it is essential to know what is planned across the curriculum which will make new or heavy demands on the library provision. If a different geographical area or a new period of history is about to be introduced, the library has to try to meet the demand.

Knowing beforehand might involve asking the child librarians to do a survey of what sorts of books children think would complement current stock. Rather than taking teachers to bookshops for first-hand choosing, it might help to take the children, for real consumer choice. Obviously, everyone cannot go, but to take a group charged with the job of selecting for their school is example of giving pupils real responsibility. It is more than a case of just gathering up a few children and nipping off to the bookshop, it can be an opportunity for purposeful curriculum work from planning through to evaluating.

Introducing new books

It is so easy to make a big splash when new books arrive, to show all the lovely, glossy treasures and hope everyone enjoys them. This is especially true when parents have been involved in fund-raising and schools want them to see something for their efforts. The problem is that the new arrivals are put on the shelves and disappear into the crowd or are borrowed and forgotten. It is better to introduce books two or three at the time, possibly once a review has been completed by a couple of child reviewers to whet the appetite. This can avoid overdose, but also constantly emphasises the importance of reading by drip feed. The library can have an almost permanent display of new arrivals with stock being updated and discussed.

Teachers' books

Good schools have lots of books for teachers. Often these are kept in the staff room, but keeping them in the school library has several effects. It shows that teachers work in a profession where reading is important and teachers do keep up to date. It also shows teachers modelling good practice in terms of being library users.

Should books go home?

Ideally, a school library is a resource that is widely available with books being used both within school and at home. In many schools this is impractical. Apart from worries about the return and care of books, the problem of books being unavailable within school when stocks are limited, has to be set against a wholesale class borrowing commitment. Many schools have a section of their library specifically for home loan. Others have specific days of the week when parents are encouraged to take their selected book home as opposed to the books that have been prescribed. It gives an odd message about reading if different versions are applied to different books at different times. This can give the impression that some reading matters and other reading is not so important; a 'take it or leave it' approach.

The local library

Schools should definitely encourage children to use the local public library. They need to see that what happens at their school mirrors what the 'grown ups' do. Regular visits, from the early days in school, with parents encouraged to join in, promote the best attitudes to reading. Even if only a proportion become library users for life, it is a start for them. Local libraries provide a source of books which children can borrow and bring for use in school, but this opportunity is rarely taken.

Schools should try to establish a good relationship with their local library, to mutual advantage. Libraries are usually delighted to receive displays of children's work about books and it is worth trying to provide some reviews in the library itself.

Chapter 18   Useful resources for teachers

Developing professional knowledge

Not so Simple Picture Books — Developing responses to Literature with 4–12 year olds
(Pam Badderley and Chris Edershaw) *Trentham* Books
The authors show how complex issues of relationships and layerings of subtext in books can extend children's understanding and thinking.

The Reading Book
(Myra Barrs and Anne Thomas) *Centre for Language in Primary Education*
A teachers' guide to learning to read. Part One surveys what we know about the reading process, the child, parent, teacher and text. Part Two is a practical guide outlining the issues and elements that make up a primary school's reading policy.

The Core Book, CLPE
A Structured Approach to Using Books Within the Reading Curriculum, *CLPE*
The Core Book discusses the use of children's books as a central resource within a structured approach to literacy development and reading in the primary school. Model lessons using the best of children's literacy. **The Core Book Guide** is published separately and lists recommend children's books.

Teaching Literacy — Balancing Perspectives
(Roger Beard) (ed) *Hodder and Stoughton*
Prominent contributors at the heart of the debate about
methods of teaching literacy look at literacy development and
attempt to lead readers toward a balanced perspective.

Spelling in Context
(Margaret Donaldson)
Seems to be out of print! But if you are lucky may find a copy.

**Reading Under Control — Teaching Reading in the Primary
School**
(Judith Graham and Alison Kelly) (ed) *David Fulton*
The book's aim is to help teachers create a rich environment
for reading and develop a principled and secure understanding
of processes and practices. The authors place the teaching of
reading in a theoretical, political and historical framework and
present a balanced coverage of all key issues. Particularly
suitable for initial and inservice training.

The Reading for Real Handbook
(Colin Harrison and Martin Coles) (ed) *Routledge*
Emphasising literature, meaning making and enjoyment, an
account of current theories underpinning reading and the
teaching of reading, with guidance on how to implement
theory into practice.

**Differently Literate — Boys, Girls and the Schooling of
Literacy**
(Dr Elaine Millard) *Falmer Press*
Combining practical research with theoretical debate, this is a
study of gender and literacy. There is an analysis of differences
of attitudes between boys and girls to reading and writing,
children's own reading choices and the impact of computers
on our understanding of gender and literacy development.
Recommendations are made for the development of cross-
curricular literacy policies.

The Teaching of Reading
(Jenny Riley) *Paul Chapman*
The book draws upon research literature to set out a practical
programme for teaching reading. The theory is shown to

support effective teaching and the author presents a genuine understanding of literacy process — showing the child's progress from early literacy through to a fully developed fluent reader. Although the study is at Key Stage 1, the book offers a valuable insight for language coordinators.

First Steps
Researched and developed by the Education Department of Western Australia
UK — Heinemann, Madeleine Lindley Ltd and UKRA.
First Steps provides a framework for linking assessment with teaching and learning. Covering four areas of **Oral Language, Reading, Writing** and **Spelling**, *First Steps* identifies milestones in children's growth and development. By analysing children's work with reference to the continua, every child's development can be assessed and monitored.

There are four books for the **Developmental Continua**, each of which provides a sensitive diagnostic framework to link the pupil's current levels of development with appropriate practical teaching strategies. There are also four **Resource Books** to expand on the teaching suggestions and provide many more practical teaching ideas. The **Parents as Partners** booklet outlines the approach and summarises the continua.

Extending Literacy — Children reading and writing non-fiction
(David Wray and Maureen Lewis) *Routledge*
This books addresses the concerns of how well children's literacy skills are extended once they have mastered the basics of literacy and how effectively they interact with non-fiction books. The authors cover in detail many useful teaching strategies and approaches which have been developed in collaboration with primary school teachers.

Literacy Assessment — Key Stage 2
(David Wray and Mary Sullivan) *Scholastic*
A structure for teacher assessment, developing school policies, involving children in monitoring their progress and preparing permanent records of children's progress for both school and parents.

Developing classroom practice

Patterns of Learning — The Primary Language Record and The National Curriculum
(Myra Barrs, Sue Ellis, Hilary Hester and Anne Thomas)
Centre for Language in Primary Education An illustration of ways of working in primary classrooms, showing teachers using the Primary Language Record and the PLR Reading Fluency Scales to gather evidence of children's progress and to inform their teaching of the National Curriculum for English.

To Rhyme or Not to Rhyme? Teaching Children to Write Poetry
(Sandy Brownjohn) *Hodder and Stoughton, 1994*
A structured approach to teaching poetry, with an abundance of methods and practice to enhance the whole English programme. This is an omnibus edition of previously published material and new chapters of activities, poems and information.

Working With Your Children — Core Guides
(Ben Brunwin and Mike Smith) *Madeleine Lindley Ltd*
Seven core guides offering teachers transferable process approaches to Literacy Development at both Key Stage 1 and 2. A fund of generic ideas and learning strategies — the authors offer day courses by working with teachers and their children in a 'Laboratory Classroom'.
- Reading Response — Fiction
- Reading for Information
- 'Telling your Story', *from inspiration to publication*
- Making your Case
- Poetry for All
- Learning through Drama
- Organising for Oracy, *the visitor, the community and the cultural journalism concept.*

Read and Retell
(Brian Cambourne and Hazel Brown) *Heinemann US and Madeleine Lindley Ltd*
Details a simple and easy-to-prepare strategy that teachers can use in the whole-language classroom — 'the retelling procedure'. Thirty-eight texts provide a range of descriptive,

persuasive, argumentative, explanatory and instructive writing, and are presented with detailed instructions for their use in the retelling context. These texts are photocopiable for classroom use.

Tell Me
(Aidan Chambers) *Thimble Press*
Practical information about book-talking in the classroom, explaining some of the processes and outlining the ground rules developed by experienced practitioners. A framework has been formulated on 'a repertoire of questions that assist readers in speaking out their reading'.

The Reading Environment — How Adults Help Children Enjoy Books
(Aidan Chambers) *Thimble Press*
Practical advice and comment on what can be done in schools to help children become thoughtful willing readers. Chapters on *The Reading Circle, Book Stocks, Displays, Reading Areas, Reading Time, Storytelling* . . . and more.

Writing for Life
(John Collerson) (ed) *PETA Australia*
Support for the argument that children should be taught to write in the various kinds of writing that are needed in the course of their education and their lives. These accounts of classroom experiences demonstrate that different genres of writing can be taught within a process writing framework.

What's Your Purpose? Reading Strategies for Non-fiction Texts
(Tish Creenaune and Lorraine Rowles) *PETA Australia and Madeleine Lindley Ltd*
A practical classroom resource for teachers across all primary years that focuses on reading non-fiction texts. Descriptions and worked examples of a number of strategies to assist pupils in becoming more effective and purposeful readers of non-fiction along with outlines for seven units of work with photocopiable pages.

Learning in an Electronic World
(Toni Downes and Cherryl Fatouros) *PETA Australia*
For teachers who have not yet started using computers as part of their classroom English teaching, through to experienced

computer users who are keen to extend their range of text types and the variety of learning experiences. A generous selection of classroom stories illustrate successful ideas for using computers in a diverse range of language learning situations.

Sustained Silent Reading in Theory and Practice
(Geoff Fenwick) *Geoff Fenwick and Madeleine Lindley Ltd*
Written to help establish the basic principles of SSR, to identify possible difficulties in its organisation and to indicate effective practice.

Library Alive! Promoting Reading and Research in the School Library
(Gwen Gawith) *A & C Black*
An invaluable resource book for teacher/librarian, packed with ideas and activities to help children learn the skills they need to become confident readers and users of books. Includes games and activities to encourage critical and evaluative skills, research using many kinds of books and knowledge and organisation of the library.

Reading Alive!
(Gwen Gawith) *A & C Black*
Activities designed to encourage reading, analysis and discussion, and to increase children's enjoyment of a variety of books.

Cracking Good Books
(Judith Graham) *NATE 1997*
A valuable resource for planning literacy sessions for junior children with an introduction to 24 children's books covering a range of different types of literature, photocopiable pupil pages, record keeping and response sheets. Each book is described in detail, with the story structure and outline, setting, era, language, genre and character.

Writing Frames — Scaffolding Children's Non-fiction Writing in a Range of Genres
(Maureen Lewis and David Wray) *University of Reading*
A outline of the characteristics of six different non-fiction genres with blank templates which can be used to support children's writing in each of these genres.

Developing Children's Non-fiction Writing — Working with Writing Frames
(Maureen Lewis and David Wray) *Scholastic Professional Bookshelf*
This book shows how children's writing can be made more purposeful and structured by using Writing Frames and offers an effective way to solve the problem of pupil's copying chunks from reference books.

I See What You Mean — Children at Work with Visual Information
(Steve Moline) *Addison Wesley, Longman, Australia and Madeleine Lindley Ltd*
The real world of reference texts offers information in images as well as in words. Examples of visual texts include maps, diagrams, time lines, graphs and tables, among others. Practical activity-laden resource book outlining learning/literacy strategies that require students to communicate using visual texts.

Exploring Poetry
NATE
(to be written)

Primary English Schemes of Work
London Borough of Tower Hamlets Advisory Team 1997
A document that can be used at different levels and adapted to the needs of individual schools and teachers, this is a ring-binder divided into five sections labelled **Introduction**, **Story**, **Non-fiction**, **Poetry**, **Appendix**. Key experiences for English are described and there are lesson plans, recommended texts, planning sheets and a glossary of terms.

Eager Readers Analysed
Teaching and Learning Strategies for Reading Using Laminated Big-books
(Alex Williams) *Madeleine Lindley Ltd*
Eager Readers Analysed offers ways of observing and assessing children's present levels of understanding and shows ways of demonstrating how the enlarged text offers a structured framework for literacy lessons. Covers in detail many areas of reading, writing, wordplay, grammar and writing forms.

Resource books for the classroom

Belair
The Belair series — Books to support English at Key Stage 2

Tales for Topics, *Belair*
Linking favourite stories e.g. *Dogger*, *Jolly Postman*, *Spot*, *Flat Stanley* and *Happy Families* with popular topics. Useful for both Key Stages 1 and 2.

Paint a Poem
Moira Andrew
Imaginative ideas for the writing and presentation of poetry for children five to eleven.

Language in Colour
Moira Andrew
Poetry starting-points for fourteen themes, all related to the environment and each introduced by a page of poetry.

Brainwaves
Brainwaves offer a range of activities which require active thinking. They have non-narrative type layouts offering a miscellany of 'ready to use' presentations which could be selected for individual or group work when part of, or linked to, an overall structured lesson plan, theme or topic.

Several English titles suitable for inclusion in a resource bank for Key Stage 2 English —
- **Writing for Different Purposes** — diaries, adverts, instructions, design, plans, diagrams and more
- **Reading for Information** — exploring different types of text
- **Comprehension** — activity sheets to encourage literal, re-organisational, inferential and evaluative and appreciative responses. **Comprehension 2 and 3** for lower and upper juniors respectively.
- **Speaking and Listening**
- **Creative Writing 2 and 3**
- **Grammar 2** — parts of speech, nouns and pronouns, adjectives, adverbs, verbs and sentence building, dialogue, punctuation.

- ■ **Communications**
- ■ **Poetry 7–11** — a collection of resource sheets and notes on twenty ways to teach poetry. The range includes action rhymes, shape poems, tongue twisters, jokes, limericks, conversation poems, adverts and ballads. (Photocopiable resource)

Blueprints, *Stanley Thornes*
Practical resource to be used either as a core English resource or as a flexible ideas bank. Teacher Resource Books contain schemes and practical ideas and Pupil Copymaster books provide photocopiable activities and assessment materials.

Titles include —
Comprehension — over 100 copiable worksheets from basic picture comprehension to Key Stage 2 assessment practice. Material from a variety of genres, including fiction, non-fiction, poetry, journalism, advertising and public information.
Also available **English at Key Stage 2** and **The Grammar and Punctuation Book (6–11)** (Photocopiable pages).

Channel 4 Schools — Videos and Teachers' Book Guides
Channel 4 and also available through Madeleine Lindley
Strong support for developing pupils' enthusiasm, independent and reflective reading, listening and speaking skills in English and a route into giving pupils opportunities to enjoy literature and study it in some detail. Videos and teacher notes for
Bill's New Frock — Anne Fine
Children of Winter — Bernie Doherty
Cliffhanger — Jacqueline Wilson
Grandpa Chatterji — Jamila Gavin
Pigeon Summer — Ann Turnbull
Thief — Majorie Blackman

Curriculum Bank, *Scholastic*
A practical, activity-based series which can be used as a planning tool when devising a comprehensive scheme of work and bank of ideas. Lesson plans, photocopiable worksheets, guidance for differentiation and formative assessment, ICT applications and cross-curricular links. The four Key Stage 2 English titles are

- **Reading Key Stage 2 — George Hunt —** covers environmental print, narrative, poetry, information and instructional texts. Built in differentiation, activities for assessment and many links with children's books. Whole class sessions and group and individual task suggested.
- **Writing**
- **Speaking and Listening — David Orme and Moira Andrew** — a variety of contexts and purposes within which children can practise key skills, responding to different audiences and using appropriate language. Arranged in sections covering information handling, explaining and understanding, reasoning and speculating, opinion and persuasion, storytelling and performance and extending vocabulary.
- **Spelling and Phonics Key Stage 1 — Liz Laycock and Anne Washtell** A range of activities to increase children's knowledge of the alphabet and phonological awareness, and to build on these to develop recognition and use of conventional spelling patterns. An emphasis on using well-structured and progressive activities within the wider perspective of children's everyday reading and writing experiences.
- **Key Stage 2** draws on existing phonic and spelling knowledge to develop skills within reading and writing and the activities linked form a clear progression from inexperience to experience. The contexts are lively and relevant to encourage an enthusiasm for language, its history, its form and its use. Photocopiable pages.

Fairytale Comprehension 1, 2 and 3
Helen Thygesen, *Addison Wesley Longman, Australia*
(*UK Madeleine Lindley Ltd*)
Each of the three books has the text of ten stories, complete with photocopiable activity pages which make up units of work. Diverse activities can be used with children of different reading and writing confidence. Skill and concept index and monitoring provision. The work becomes progressively more challenging through books 1, 2 and 3.

How to be Brilliant at — series
Each book contains copiable sheets for juniors aimed at developing processes and skills. **Writing** focuses on the writing

process, idea gathering, redrafting and provides story ideas: **Spelling** offers word and sound play, puzzles and games; **Grammar** looks at parts of speech, alphabetisation, punctuation. **Making Books** provides copiable ideas and instruction sheets for junior classrooms (Photocopiable pages).

Ideas Bank
various authors *Folens*
Teacher books in the **Ideas Bank** series offer a *combination* of photocopiable activity pages for children, along with background information, extra ideas and teaching strategies. There is a range of titles across various subject areas. Particularly useful for English at Key Stage 2 are —

■ **Reading in Context 2** (Pat Hughes) which offers lots of starting points using children's books written in various forms — narrative, poetry, picture books, fantasy, realism, history, information and community texts. Also ideas for classroom and library activities for groups and individuals.

■ **Encouraging Reading — Junior** (Richard Brown) which has ideas and activities for children who have some independence in reading and who are exploring texts and books.

■ **Writing to Communicate** (Christopher Webster) emphasises the communicative aspect of writing, encouraging different writing techniques across a range of curricular ideas.

■ **Telling Stories** (Louis Fidge) presents a framework for developing story telling and writing in different styles and genres through supportive collaboration in planning, editing, drafting and presentation.

■ **Information and Library Skills — Books 1 and 2** (Richard Brown) Twenty-two activities to develop skills needed when sourcing and reading a range of non-fiction — understanding classification, using information books conventions, posing questions, note-taking and more. The two books show how to set a purpose, ways into activities and offer development and extension. The subjects covered cross various curricular areas and are more challenging in Book 2.

■ **Poetry 7–11** A resource of complete poems and rhymes, with linked activities and supported with an abundance of teacher ideas for all aspects of poetry reading, writing and speaking.

■ **Punctuation** (Chris Webster) The Ideas Bank regular format, with teacher prompts, activity ideas, copiable pages for independent and group work. Junior focus.

Inspirations *Scholastic*
Series which aims to balance current theory with creative classroom-tested practice, outlining knowledge on topic and providing teaching strategies and advice on assessment and recording. English titles currently useful are **Inspirations for Writing** and **Inspirations for Grammar**.

Keys into . . . *Addison Wesley Longman, Australia (UK through Madeleine Lindley Ltd)*
Lesson plans and modelling strategies, with blackline masters, to assist teachers to develop the language programme from a literature base. Whole class modelling, group and independent activities.
There are three **Keys into** . . . titles which are based on *First Steps* approaches: **Key into Fairytales, Folktales and Fables; Keys into Fantasy**; and **Keys into Picture Books**.

Read and Respond, *Scholastic*
The Read and Respond series is designed to deepen children's understanding of popular and well-written books by significant children's authors. Interactive photcopiable worksheets to encourage children to think critically, justify preferences and discuss viewpoints other than their own. Before, during and after reading activities and specific reading skill development opportunities. There are currently 6 titles in this series —

Beginner (7–9 year olds)	*Oi! Get off our Train*	*Amazing Grace*
Intermediate (8–10 years)	*Fair's Fair*	*The Suitcase Kid*
Advanced (9–11 years)	*The Sheep Pig*	*The Secret Garden*

Responding to the Traditional Tales KS2, *Evans*
Copiable editions of 9 myths (including 8 Greek myths) with planning ideas and activity sheets.

Language and Literacy Lessons on Video

Guided Reading for Fluent Readers

Part One shows a group of 8–9 year olds in a guided reading session with their teacher and Part Two shows an approach to guided reading with 11–13 year olds. Each lesson is covered in about 15 minutes of video time, and the overall cassette lasts 40 minutes. Origin — New Zealand

Reciprocal Teaching: Extending Reading Strategies

This 18-minute video explains the principles of reciprocal teaching, an interactive teaching technique involving strategies which readers can learn to apply independently. A teacher and her students are seen using the system with a scientific article from a school journal. The resource includes a booklet with notes for teachers. Origin — New Zealand

Creating a Community of Readers — Part 2

A video package that looks at the role of literature in children's reading. In **Part 2** the teacher's existing practice is shown and developed by the introduction of 'reading circles' in which groups of six or so children begin to learn how to discuss particular works of literature. The video follows the progress of a particular group of children over two terms. Running time — 1 hour. Origin — Brighton UK

Index

ORDER FORM

Post: *Customer Services Department, Falmer Press, Rankine Road, Basingstoke, Hampshire, RG24 8PR*
Tel: *(01256) 813000* Fax: *(01256) 479438*
E-mail: *book.orders@tandf.co.uk*

10% DISCOUNT AND FREE P&P FOR SCHOOLS OR INDIVIDUALS ORDERING THE COMPLETE SET ORDER YOUR SET NOW. WITH CREDIT CARD PAYMENTS, YOU WON'T BE CHARGED TILL DESPATCH.

TITLE	DUE	ISBN	PRICE	QTY
SUBJECT LEADERS' HANDBOOKS SET		**(RRP £207.20)**	**£185.00**	
Coordinating Science	2/98	0 7507 0688 0	£12.95	
Coordinating Design and Technology	2/98	0 7507 0689 9	£12.95	
Coordinating Maths	2/98	0 7507 0687 2	£12.95	
Coordinating Physical Education	2/98	0 7507 0693 7	£12.95	
Coordinating History	2/98	0 7507 0691 0	£12.95	
Coordinating Music	2/98	0 7507 0694 5	£12.95	
Coordinating Geography	2/98	0 7507 0692 9	£12.95	
Coordinating English at Key Stage 1	4/98	0 7507 0685 6	£12.95	
Coordinating English at Key Stage 2	4/98	0 7507 0686 4	£12.95	
Coordinating IT	4/98	0 7507 0690 2	£12.95	
Coordinating Art	4/98	0 7507 0695 3	£12.95	
Coordinating Religious Education	Late 98	0 7507 0613 9	£12.95	
Management Skills for SEN Coordinators	Late 98	0 7507 0697 X	£12.95	
Building a Whole School Assessment Policy	Late 98	0 7507 0698 8	£12.95	
Curriculum Coordinator and OFSTED Inspection	Late 98	0 7507 0699 6	£12.95	
Coordinating Curriculum in Smaller Primary School	Late 98	0 7507 0700 3	£12.95	

Value of Books	
P&P*	
Total	

I wish to pay by:

❑ Cheque *(Pay Falmer Press)*
❑ Pro-forma invoice
❑ Credit Card *(Mastercard / Visa / AmEx)*

*Please add p&p
orders up to £25 — *10%*
orders from £25 to £50 — *5%*
orders over £50 — *free*

Card Number _____ Expiry Date _____
Signature _____
Name _____ Title/Position _____
School _____
Address _____
_____
Postcode _____ Country _____
Tel no. _____ Fax _____
E-mail _____

❑ If you do not wish to receive further promotional information from the Taylor&Francis Group, please tick box.

All prices are correct at time of going to print but may change without notice

Ref: 1197BFSLAD